# Learning to Re...
# Using Phonics

**Author**
Mara Ellen Guckian

**Editor in Chief**
Brent L. Fox, M. Ed.

**Creative Director**
Sarah M. Fournier

**Cover Artist**
Diem Pascarella

**Illustrator**
Kevin Cameron

**Art Coordinator**
Renée Mc Elwee

**Imaging**
Amanda R. Harter

**Publisher**
Mary D. Smith, M.S. Ed.

**Teacher Created Resources**
12621 Western Avenue
Garden Grove, CA 92841
*www.teachercreated.com*
ISBN: 978-1-4206-1708-5

©2022 Teacher Created Resources
Reprinted, 2022

Made in U.S.A.

For standards correlations, visit
*http://www.teachercreated.com/standards/.*

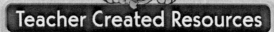

**Teacher Created Resources**

# Table of Contents

# Introduction

The *Learning to Read Using Phonics* series was developed to help young learners improve their reading skills through phonics and other word-decoding activities.

Phonics refers to the relationship between sounds and the alphabet letter or letters that represent them. The 26 letters of the English language can represent 44 different sounds!

When decoding, the sound heard is translated to a letter or letters. For example, the word *bake* has four letters, b-a-k-e, but three sounds or phonemes: /b/ /a/ /k/. Knowing which letters make which sounds is very important. Decoding letter sounds to write and spell words correctly is a necessary tool for learning to read.

The more comfortable young readers are with identifying words, the better readers they will become. The ability to decode helps children identify words more quickly and enables them to read more fluently.

The more fluently children read, the better their comprehension and the more likely it is that reading will be an enjoyable pastime.

## Practice Tips

1. Read to your child as often as possible. Encourage them to read to you as well.

2. Guide young readers to sound out new words using the phonics skills they are learning.

3. Rhyme words to create lists of words with similar endings. Pick a word ending and add different beginning letters or blends. Start with endings such as *at*—bat, cat…, or *ing*—bring, sing, string, wing. Write them down, or recite them while walking or traveling in the car. Make a game of it. Nonsense words are okay. The goal is to notice the matching ending sounds.

4. When reading, notice how different a letter can sound in different words, such as the soft *g* in *giraffe* as compared to the hard *g* in *goat*.

5. Practice writing words as they are learned. Perhaps your child(ren) can write a list of words with the same beginning or ending sound or label a drawing they made.

6. Try decoding big words for fun. Point out a big word such as *caterpillar* (cat-er-pil-lar) that you see in a story or on a sign. Ask, "What little words do you see hiding in the big word?" (cat, pill). Blend all the word parts together, and try to read the word.

Enjoy exploring sounds, decoding and reading with your young learners. Make it fun!

# How to Use This Book

Picture clues are provided in this book to help students focus on naming each item and then sounding it out. Words and letters in this book are often written in gray so that students can trace them to continue practicing proper letter formation. Tracing also helps reinforce spelling as more and more words are learned.

The different sections of this book follow a natural progression to help young readers and writers develop a solid phonics foundation. The activities are presented to allow young learners to identify sounds, letters, and words. From there, they can proceed to sounding out printed words (decoding) and writing words and sentences (encoding).

Students need opportunities to practice new phonics skills on a regular basis. Word decoding is a skill they will be using for many years as they transition from *learning to read* to *reading to learn*. Activities are presented in the following sequence:

- First, students are provided with a review of beginning and ending consonant sounds.

- Practice is expanded to include hard and soft *c* and *g* consonant sounds followed by words with double letters at the end or in the middle.

- A review of short vowels leads into a study of the more complex sounds of r-controlled vowels.

- Long vowels and the sounds of *y* are reviewed, and more detailed practice is provided as students' word-decoding skills improve.

- Next, beginning and ending consonant blends are addressed in detail. Being able to blend sounds into words is a very important component when learning to read fluently and to spell correctly.

- Attention is then focused on digraphs, trigraphs, and silent letters.

- Finally, long vowel teams and unusual vowel sounds are examined. Like sight words, these combinations need to be practiced to be learned.

- Use the Answer Key (pages 109–112) as a guide to what each picture could represent. The goal, in phonics, is to identify the correct sound in order to determine the correct letter. Ask what the picture is before saying that an answer is incorrect. A different answer may still be an acceptable response. If, for instance, your child sees a picture of a *dog* on a "D" page, and says it begins with a "p" because it is a *puppy*, that is ok. Their answer depends upon the sound they hear. You might then ask, "What letter would it begin with if it was a *dog*?"

*Note:* Check out the "Phonics Words to Know" on page 5 to review terms often used in phonics study.

# Phonics Words to Know

**Blends** occur when two consonants come together in a word and each letter's sound is heard separately, but the two sounds "blend" together. Consonant blends are sometimes called "clusters."
*Example*: In the word **<u>sl</u>ide**, both the **s** and the **l** sounds are heard.

**Consonants** include the 21 letters of the alphabet that are not vowels—
b, c, d, f, g, h, j, k, l, m, n, p, q, r, s, t, v, w, x, y (sometimes), and z.

**Decoding** refers to knowing the sounds letters make and using them to sound out words.
*Example*: The letter **t** makes the /t/ sound, which is pronounced "tuh."

**Digraphs** occur when two letters come together to make one speech sound:

- A **consonant digraph** is a single sound made by two consonants such as *ch, sh,* or *th.*
  *Example:* In the word **<u>sh</u>oe**, the **s** and **h** combine to make the /sh/ sound, as if you are telling someone to be quiet, "Shhh!"

- A **vowel digraph** is a single sound represented by two vowels. Often, the first vowel is heard and the second vowel is silent.
  *Examples:* **ai** in p<u>ai</u>l, **ay** in pl<u>ay</u>, **ea** in b<u>ea</u>ch, **ie** in p<u>ie</u>, **oa** in b<u>oa</u>t
  The vowel digraphs **oo** and **ow** can make different sounds.
  *Examples:* h<u>oo</u>k or h<u>oo</u>p; c<u>ow</u> or rainb<u>ow</u>

**Encoding** refers to the printing or writing of letters and words.

**Fluency** is the ability to read comfortably with speed, accuracy, and expression.

**Phoneme** refers to a single sound; the smallest unit of spoken language.
*Example:* cart has four letters, but only three sounds: /c/ /ar/ /t/.

**Phonemic awareness** is the ability to isolate sounds.

**R-controlled**, or "bossy r", sounds occur when the letter **r** follows a vowel, which causes the sound of the vowel to change.
*Examples:* Say "cat" and listen to the sound the letter **a** makes. Then say "car" and listen to that **a** sound. Do you hear the difference? The **r** that follows the **a** in "car" changes the sound of the **a**.

**Syllables** are word parts. Every syllable in a word contains one vowel or the letter **y**.
*Examples:* *fly* has 1 syllable    *car-rot* has 2 syllables    *ba-na-na* has 3 syllables

**Trigraph**—A trigraph is a single sound represented by three letters.
*Example:* Listen to the sound the letters **str** make in <u>str</u>ing.

**Vowels**—The alphabet letters known as vowels are **a, e, i, o, u**, and sometimes **y**. Every word in the English language has a vowel in it.
Long vowels say their names. Short vowel sounds usually occur when a word has one vowel between two consonants. (s<u>a</u>t, r<u>u</u>n, b<u>e</u>d)

**Rhyme**—Words with the same ending sounds such as *bell, fell,* and *sell* are called rhyming words. Groups of these words form word "families."

Name: _____

# Consonant Match

**Directions:** Listen to the **beginning sound** of each item. Draw lines to match each item to its beginning consonant.

Name: _____

# Write the Beginning Sound

**Directions:** Listen to the **beginning sound** of each item. Write the beginning letter and trace the rest of each word. Read the words.

_____ art

_____ um

_____ op

_____ ip

_____ an

_____ un

_____ eet

_____ ive

_____ oat

_____ ion

_____ unny

_____ ilk

Name: _____

# Choose the Beginning Sound

**Directions:** Listen to the **beginning sound** of each item.  Circle the consonant that makes each beginning sound.

s  n  z  w

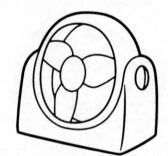

f  m  t  s

n  d  h  s

b  d  k  t

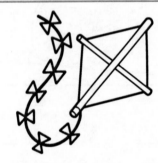

k  t  l  z

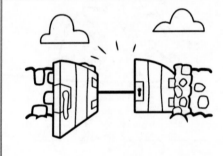

c  t  g  p

l  p  m  b

g  r  s  n

n  v  w  g

**Directions:** Write three words you know that begin with the letter **d**.

_____  _____  _____

- - - - - - - - - - - - - - -  - - - - - - - - - - - - - - -  - - - - - - - - - - - - - - -

_____  _____  _____

Name: _____

# Listen and Rhyme

**Directions:** Listen to the **beginning sound** of each item. Write the beginning letter and trace the rest of each word. Read the words.

ug

ig

ut

ig

ug

ut

**Directions:** Look at the words you completed above. Write the pairs of rhyming words in the boxes below.

| | | |
|---|---|---|
| _____ rhymes with _____ | _____ rhymes with _____ | _____ rhymes with _____ |

Name: _____

# Beginning Sound Match

**Directions:** Name each item. Circle the two items in each box that have the same **beginning sound**. Cross out the item that has a different beginning sound.

Name: _____

# Listen and Match

**Directions:** Listen for each **beginning consonant sound**. Draw lines to match each pair of items with the same beginning sound.

# Hard C Sound

**Directions:** The **hard c** sound is like the **c** in *cat*. Add a **c** to the beginning of each word. Read each word. Circle the items that begin with a **hard c** sound.

__astle    __ube    __ereal    __ar

**Directions:** Trace each sentence. Circle the words that have a **hard c** sound.

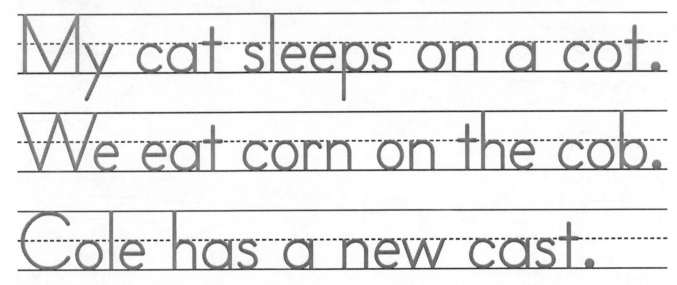

My cat sleeps on a cot.

We eat corn on the cob.

Cole has a new cast.

**Directions:** Read and trace each **hard c** word. Clap out the syllables. Then circle the correct number of syllables for each word.

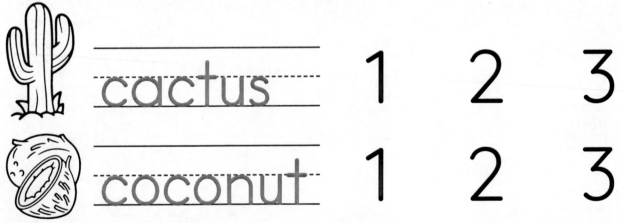

cactus    1    2    3

coconut    1    2    3

Name: _____

# Soft C Sound

**Directions:** The **soft c** sound is like the **c** in *cent.* Read and trace each word. Circle the items that have a **soft c** sound. Cross out the items that have a **hard c** sound.

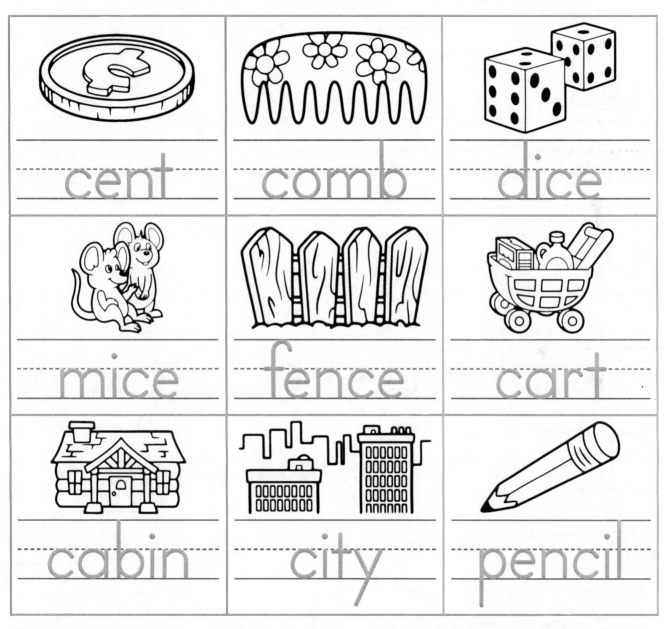

cent

comb

dice

mice

fence

cart

cabin

city

pencil

**Directions:** Listen as you read the word below. It has a **hard c** and a **soft c**. Circle each **c** and draw a line to the correct label.

bicycle

hard c

soft c

Name: _____

# Hard G Sound

**Directions:** The **hard g** sound is like the **g** in *gum*. Read and trace each word. Listen to the beginning sounds. Circle the items that begin with the **hard g** sound. Cross out the other item.

glue     gem     goat     grill

**Directions:** Trace each sentence. Circle the words that have a **hard g** sound.

The girl gave her a gift.

Mom will go get gas.

He grew green grapes.

**Directions:** Read and trace each **hard g** word. Clap out the syllables and circle the correct number of syllables for each word.

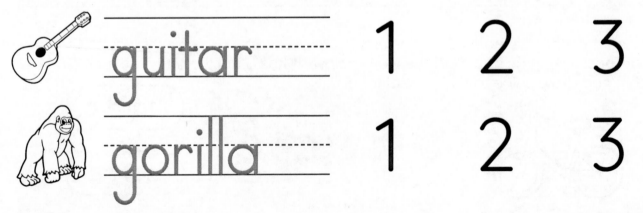

guitar     1   2   3

gorilla     1   2   3

Name: _____

# Soft G Sound

**Directions:** The **soft g** sound is like the **g** in *magic*. Follow the directions under each hand. Listen to the sound of each **soft g** word as you read it.

Draw some **germs** on the left hand.

Draw some **gems** on the right hand.

**Directions:** Trace each sentence. Circle the words that have a **soft g** sound. Did you find all four words?

Look at that huge giraffe! It is a gentle giant.

**Directions:** Listen as you sound out the three-syllable word below. It means "very large." It has a **hard g** and a **soft g**. Circle each **g** and draw a line to the correct label.

( soft g )     gi gan tic     ( hard g )

Name: _____

# Circle the Ending

**Directions:** Listen to the ending sound of the item in each box.  Circle the ending letter for each item.

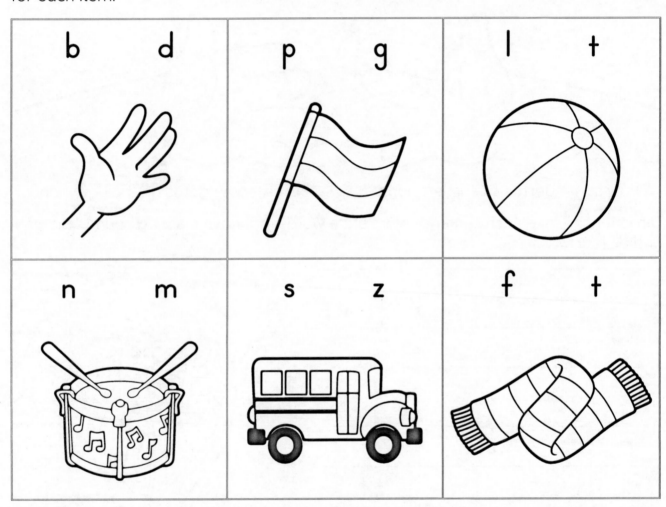

**Directions:** Write the ending consonant for the items below.  Trace and read each word.

Name: _____

# Match the Endings

**Directions:** Listen to the **ending sound** of each item.  Draw lines to match each item to its ending consonant.

p

r

s

t

x

Name: _____

# Add the Endings

**Directions:** Listen to the **ending sound** of each item. Trace the beginning letters and add the ending letter. Read each word.

Name: _____

# Same Beginning and Ending

**Directions:** Some words begin and end with the same letter. Use the pictures and middle letters as clues. Write the same beginning and ending letter for each item.

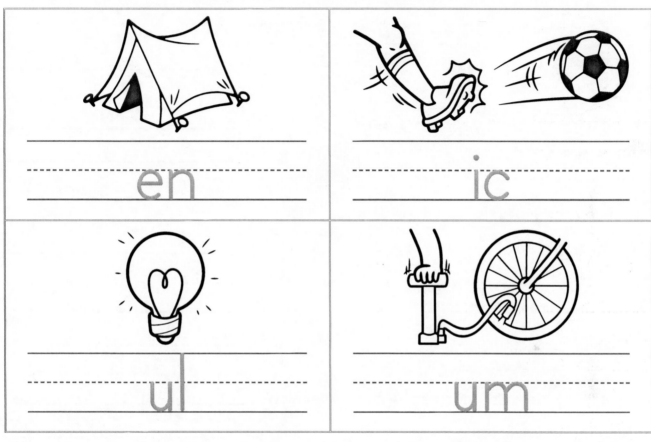

**Directions:** Use the words in the word bank that begin and end with the same letters to answer the questions.

( noon    peep    roar )

What sound does a lion make? _____

What is another way to say 12 o'clock? _____

What sound does a baby chick make? _____

Name: _____

# Double Letters -ff

**Directions:** Read each word that ends in **ff** in the word bank. Then, choose the correct word to answer each question.

> bluff   cliff   off   sniff   stiff

1. Which word is the opposite of "on?"

2. When something is hard to bend, it is

3. What is another way to say "smell"?

4. Which two words mean almost the same thing?

**Directions:** Add **ff** in the middle of the letters below to make two new words. Read the words and color the pictures.

5.  wa___le   and   mu___in

# Double Letters -ll

**Directions:** Use the word wheels to make rhyming words by adding **ll**. Read each group of rhyming words.

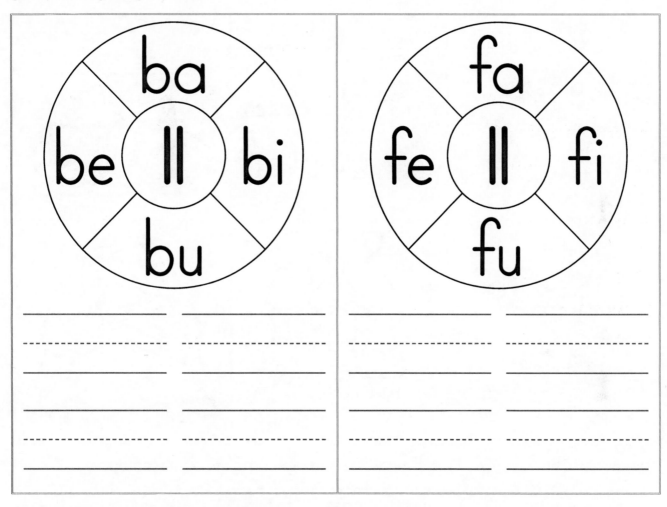

_____     _____

- - - - - - - -     - - - - - - - -

_____     _____

- - - - - - - -     - - - - - - - -

_____     _____

- - - - - - - -     - - - - - - - -

**Directions:** Add **ll** in the middle of the letters below to make new words. Read the words you make and color the pictures.

ba ___ oon

pi ___ ow

Name: _____

# Double Letters -ss

**Directions:** Read the **ss** words in each box.  Circle the one that matches the item.

**Directions:** Choose a word from the word bank to complete each sentence.

( mess   pass   recess )

1. I love to go out at _____.

2. This room is a _____!

3. He can _____ the ball.

Name: _____

# Double Letters -tt

**Directions:** Read and trace each **tt** word.  Then draw a line to its picture.

mutt

mitt

letter

litter

**Directions:** Use the words in the word bank to label each word with **tt** in the middle.

bottle    butter    button    kitten    mitten    rattle

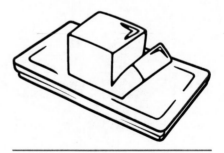

Name: _____

# Double Letters -zz

**Directions:** Write **zz** at the end of each group of letters. Read the three new words you made.

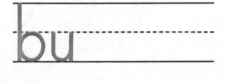

bu _____   ja _____   fi _____

**Directions:** Sometimes **zz** is in the middle of a word. Sound out the two-syllable words in the word bank. Use a word to complete each sentence. Read your sentences.

| fizzy | frizzy | fuzzy | pizza | puzzle |

1. I love to eat _____.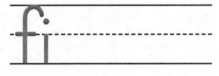

2. My blanket is _____.

3. That drink is _____.

4. Her doll's hair is so _____. 

5. He can do the _____.

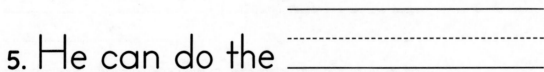

24

Name: _____

# Find the Doubles

**Directions:** Read each sentence and underline the double letter words. Then, write each double letter word in the correct row.

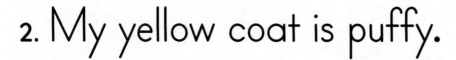

1. A kitten is on the cliff.

2. My yellow coat is puffy.

3. Toss the ball on the grass.

4. I can eat two little muffins.

5. Press all the big buttons.

**ff** _____  _____  _____

**ll** _____  _____  _____

**ss** _____  _____  _____

 **tt** _____  _____  _____

25

Name: _____

# Add a Short A or E

**Directions:** Fill in the blanks with the letter **a** to make short vowel words in the sentences. Read each sentence.

The c_t h_s a h_t.

It is a p_n!

**Directions:** Fill in the blanks with the letter **e** to make short vowel words in the sentences. Read each sentence.

I have a p_t h_n.

Its n_st is on a sl_d.

**Directions:** Name each item. Listen to the vowel sound for each item. Write an **a** or an **e** to complete each word.

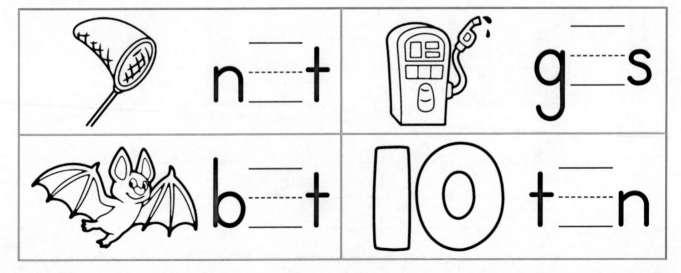

n_t        g_s

b_t        t_n

Name: _____

# I, O, or U?

**Directions:** Fill in the blanks with the letter **i** to make short vowel words. Read the sentence.

The p__g has a b__g b__b.

**Directions:** Fill in the blanks with the letter **o** to make short vowel words. Read the sentence.

The d__g g__t a m__p.

**Directions:** Fill in the blanks with the letter **u**. Read the short **u** words you made. Draw lines to match pairs of rhyming words.

 b__g

t__b

 s__b

b__n

 s__n

r__g

Name: _____

# Short A, E, I, O, or U?

**Directions:** Name each item. Choose the correct vowel to complete each short vowel word.

b __ x          n __ t          b __ t

w __ b          g __ m          l __ p

f __ n          p __ g          d __ g

f r __ g        n __ st         f __ sh

# Short Vowel Sentences

**Directions:** Read the short vowel words in the word bank. Use a word to complete each sentence. Read the sentences you made.

| log | map | net | pig | pup | rug |

1. I'll get bugs in my _____.

2. The _____ is on the wall.

3. My dog has a _____!

4. A _____ is in the mud.

5. The frog hops on a _____.

6. We can sit on a _____.

Name: _____

# R-Controlled Words -ar

**Directions:** Add **ar** to complete each **r-controlled** word. Read the words. Draw lines connecting two pairs of rhyming words.

c____t          f____          b____n

h____d          p____t          j____

**Directions:** Read the sentences and circle the words with **ar**. Listen to the sound the **ar** makes. Write the **ar** words underneath each sentence.

1. He has a shark card.

_____    _____

_____    _____

2. Will you park the car?

_____    _____

_____    _____

3. Stars glow in the dark.

_____    _____

_____    _____

4. We are at the farm.

_____    _____

_____    _____

Name: _____

# R-Controlled Words -er

**Directions:** Read each sentence and underline the words that have **er** in them. Then finish the pictures.

**1** Her fern needs water.

**2** A tower is by a river.

**Directions:** Add **er** to each word. Read the new words. How did adding **er** change the meaning of the words?

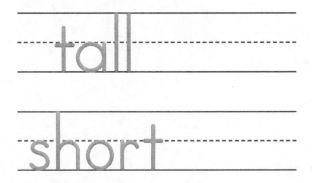

tall

short

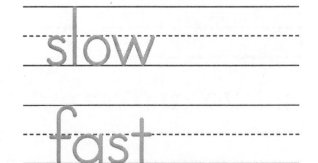

slow

fast

Name: _____

# R-Controlled Words -ir

**Directions:** Add **ir** to complete each **r-controlled** word. Read the words. Draw lines to connect the rhyming words.

sh____t       f____       b____d

st____       d____       t____   sta____

**Directions:** Read the sentences and circle the words with **ir**. Listen to the sound the **ir** makes. Write the **ir** words underneath each sentence.

1. That little bird can chirp.

_____   _____

2. She likes to twirl her skirt.

_____   _____

3. He is first, not third.

_____   _____

4. I got dirt on my shirt.

_____   _____

# R-Controlled Words -or

**Directions:** Add **or** to complete the words on the left. Read each word and draw a line to its matching picture.

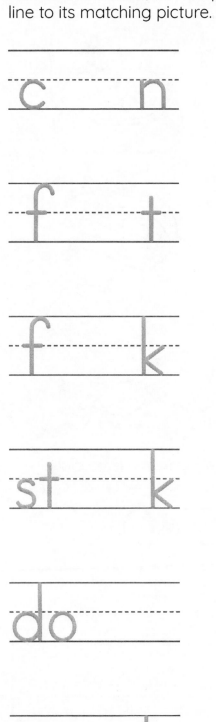

c ___ n

f ___ t

f ___ k

st ___ k

do ___

c ___ k

Name: _____

# R-Controlled Words -ur

**Directions:** Name each item. Circle two items in each column that have the **ur** sound.

**Directions:** Read the words in the word bank to find rhyming words. Listen closely. Write each pair of rhyming **ur** words in a box.

blur    four    hour    sour    spur    your

| | | |
|---|---|---|
| _____ | _____ | _____ |
| rhymes with | rhymes with | rhymes with |
| _____ | _____ | _____ |

Name: _____

# R-Controlled Vowel Review

**Directions:** Circle the correct pair of letters for each **r-controlled** word and write them on the lines. Read the words.

ir    er    ar

b___d

ar    er    or

w___m

ar    ir    er

___m

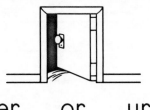

er    or    ur

do___

or    er    ir

f___n

ar    er    ur

st___

ar    or    ir

b___n

ar    er    or

f___t

or    er    ur

riv___

er    ir    ur

p___se

ar    ur    ir

g___l

ur    or    er

fing___

Name: _____

# If You Add an E...

**Directions:** Read each short-vowel word and add an **e**. Write the new long-vowel word. Use the pictures as clues for the new words.

can + [e] = _____

cap + [e] = _____

cub + [e] = _____

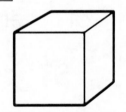

kit + [e] = _____

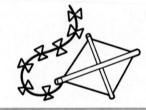

man + [e] = _____

pin + [e] = _____

tap + [e] = _____

tub + [e] = _____

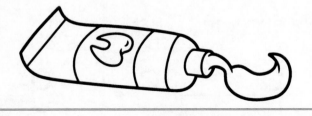

Name: _____

# Silent E Words

**Directions:** Read each word in the box. Circle the correct **silent e** word for each item. Then write the correct word under its picture.

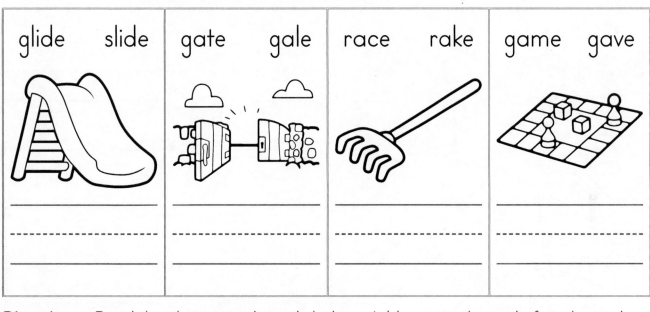

| glide  slide | gate  gale | race  rake | game  gave |
|---|---|---|---|

**Directions:** Read the short-vowel words below. Add an **e** to the end of each word. Read the new long-vowel words you made.

at          bit          cut

dim          fin          hop

**Directions:** Add an **e** to the end of the letters below. Read the word. Draw a picture of the word.

cak

Name: _____

# Long A Words

**Directions:** Use the word wheels to make **long a** word families. Write these rhyming words on the lines provided.

b
c ake f
l

_____   _____
- - - - - - - - - -   - - - - - - - - - -
_____   _____
- - - - - - - - - -   - - - - - - - - - -
_____   _____

d
g ate l
m

_____   _____
- - - - - - - - - -   - - - - - - - - - -
_____   _____
- - - - - - - - - -   - - - - - - - - - -
_____   _____

f
l ace p
r

_____   _____
- - - - - - - - - -   - - - - - - - - - -
_____   _____
- - - - - - - - - -   - - - - - - - - - -
_____   _____

Name: _____

# Long E Words

**Directions:** Most **long e** words don't have a **silent e** ending. Instead, **ee** makes the long e sound. Trace each word and draw a line to its picture.

teeth

sleep

tree

wheel

jeep

peek

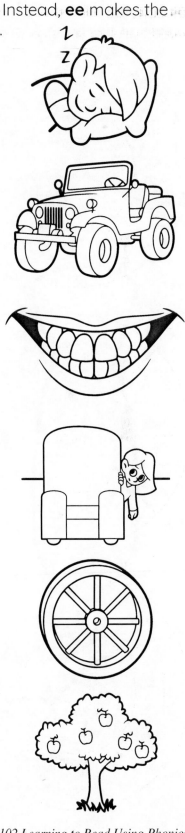

Name: _____

# Long I Words

**Directions:** All the ties have **long i** words in them. Read and trace the words in each tie. Color the ties if the two words rhyme. Do not color the ties unless the words rhyme.

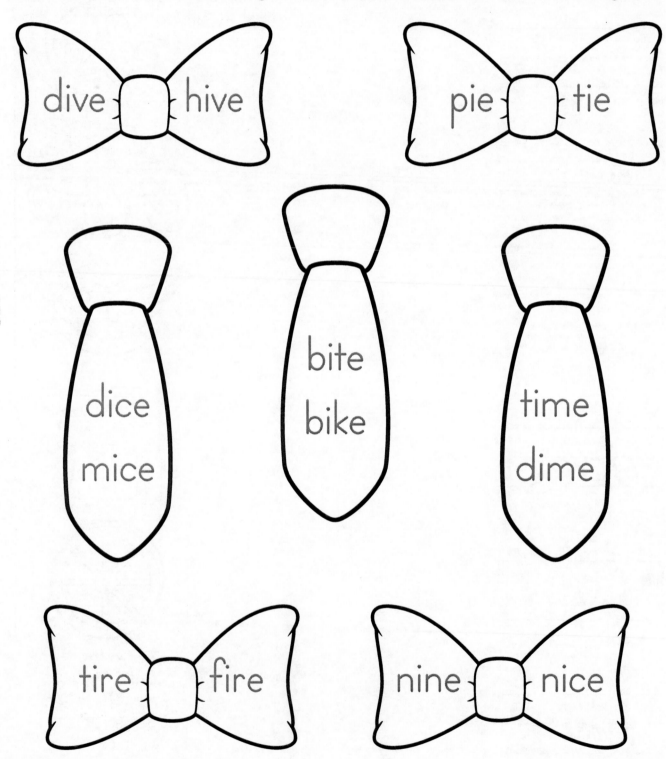

Name: _____

# Long O Words

**Directions:** Name the **long o** items in each row. Cross out the **long o** item that does not rhyme with the first item in the row.

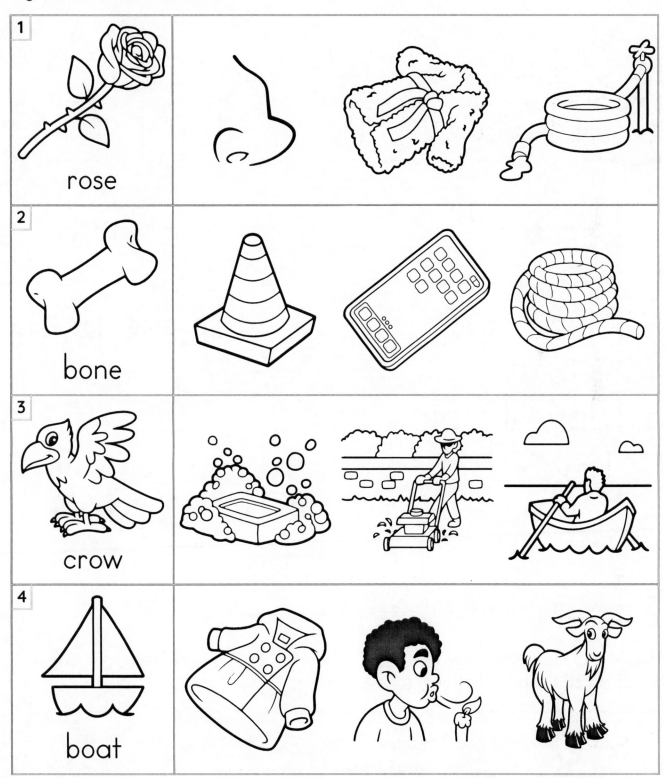

Name: _____

# Long U Words

**Directions:** The **long u** sound is spelled many different ways. Choose the correct **long u** word to complete each sentence.

| juice | tube | mule | flute | glue |

1. I saw a _____ on the farm.

2. Here is a _____ for the pool.

3. I love to play my _____.

4. You can have _____ or milk.

5. I can fix it with _____.

**Directions:** Add a **u** to each word below. <u>Underline</u> each **silent e**. Read the **long u** words. Circle the two words that rhyme.

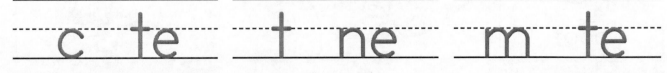

c__te    t__ne    m__te

Name: _____

# Long Vowel Sentences

**Directions:** Read and trace each sentence. Circle the two rhyming words in each one.

They pose with a rose.

The mice play with dice.

A tube is on the cube.

They will bake a cake.

Name: _____

# Y Can Sound Like I or E

## long i

**Directions:** Use the word wheel to make one-syllable words. Read the words. The **y** will have a **long i** sound.

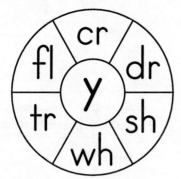

_____  _____  _____

_____  _____  _____

_____  _____  _____

## long e

**Directions:** Add a **y** to complete each two-syllable word. Read each word. The **y** will have a **long e** sound.

bunn___

lil___

part___

curl___

cit___

pon___

Name: _____

# Which Y Sound Is It?

**Directions:** Add a **y** to the end of each group of letters. Read the word and listen to the ending sound. Circle the **i** or the **e** to match each ending.

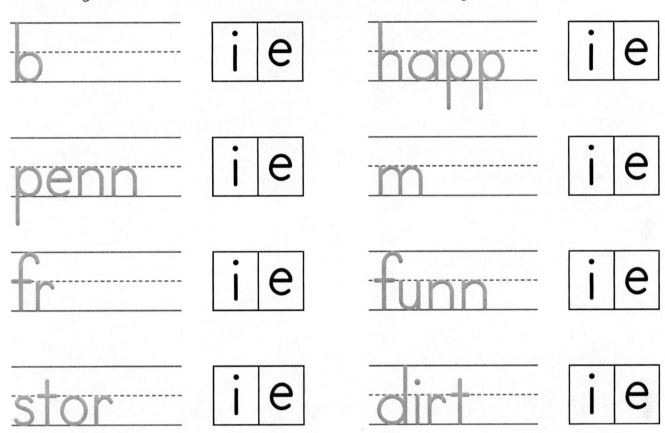

b_____ | i | e    happ_____ | i | e

penn_____ | i | e    m_____ | i | e

fr_____ | i | e    funn_____ | i | e

stor_____ | i | e    dirt_____ | i | e

**Directions:** Trace and read each word and color the pictures. Listen to the ending and circle the correct ending sound.

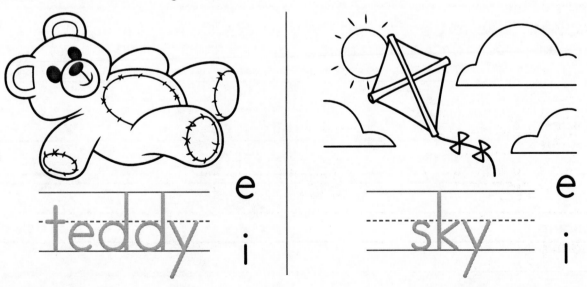

teddy    e
         i

sky    e
       i

# Fill-ins and Sorts

**Directions:** Use the picture clues to complete each sentence using a **y** word from the word bank.  Read each sentence.

kitty     try     muddy

My puppy got all
_____
__ __ __ __ __ __ __ __ !
_____ .

Why is the tiny
_____
__ __ __ __ __ __ __ __
_____ so shy?
_____
__ __ __ __ __ __ __ __

We saw the baby birds _____ to fly.

**Directions:** Circle the **y** words in the sentences above.  Choose three words that have an **e ending sound** and three words that have an **i ending sound** and write them.

| | | | |
|---|---|---|---|
| **e**<br>ending<br>sound | | | |
| **i**<br>ending<br>sound | | | |

Name: _____

# Add a Long Vowel

**Directions:** Write the long vowel to complete each two-syllable word. Read each word and clap the syllables.

cr __ yon          h __ tel          t __ ble

m __ sic          p __ per          p __ lot

t __ ger          r __ ler          sp __ der

arr __ w          r __ bot          zer __

Name: _____

# Long or Short?

**Directions:** Name the item in each box. Decide if the vowel sound is **long** or **short**. Circle your answers.

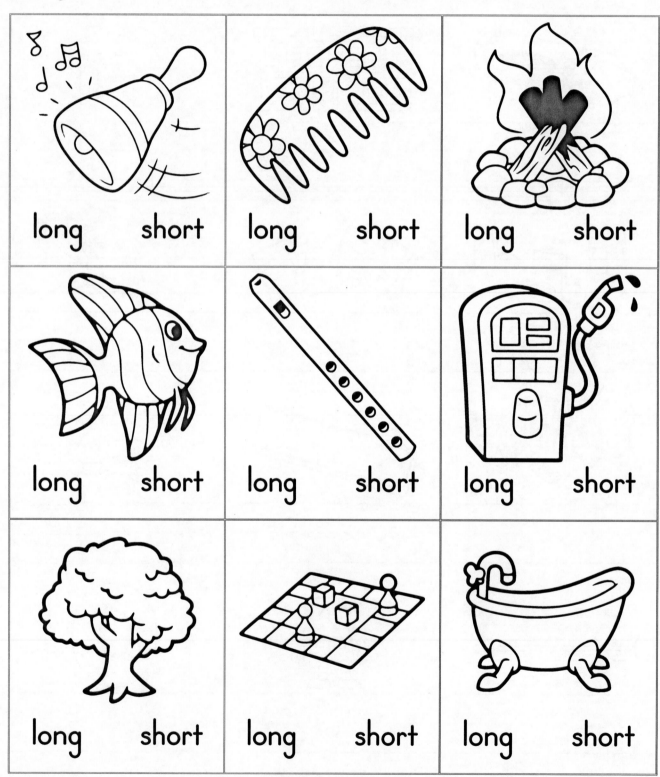

| long | short | long | short | long | short |
| long | short | long | short | long | short |
| long | short | long | short | long | short |

Name: _____

# Vowel Sort

**Directions:** Name each item.  Does it have a long-vowel sound or a short-vowel sound?
Write the word for each picture in the correct column.  Check your spelling.

| Long Vowel Sound | Short Vowel Sound |
|---|---|
| | |

Name: _____

# Beginning Bl Blends

**Directions:** Name each item. Circle the items that begin with the **bl blend**. Use a *blue* crayon. Cross out the other items.

**Directions:** Add the **bl blend** to the beginning of each group of letters. Read the words. Circle the **bl** word that is a color.

_____ ade      _____ ack      _____ og

_____ end      _____ ink      _____ oom

Name: _____

# Beginning Cl Blends

**Directions:** Add **cl** to the beginning of each group of letters. Read and trace each word.

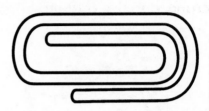

am          ap          ip

ean          oud          iff

aw          ock          ay

**Directions:** Read and trace the word.
Draw and color a face on the clown.

clown

Name: _____

# Beginning Fl Blends

**Directions:** Name each item and listen to the beginning sounds. Circle the items that begin with the **fl blend**. Cross out the other items.

**Directions:** Add the **fl blend** to the beginning of each group of letters. Read the words.

_____ ame      _____ oss      _____ ip

_____ at       _____ ew       _____ oor

Name: _____

# Beginning Gl Blends

**Directions:** Add **gl** to the beginning of each group of letters. Trace and read each word and then draw a line to the correct item.

_____ obe

_____ oves

_____ ue

**Directions:** Read and trace each **gl** word and draw a line to its match. Do you hear the **gl blend**?

glass

glasses

**Directions:** Add **gl** to the beginning of each word. Read the three words and circle the two that mean "happy."

_____ ad          _____ ide          _____ ee

Name: _____

# Beginning Pl Blends

**Directions:** Name each item. Circle the items that begin with the **pl blend**. Cross out the other items.

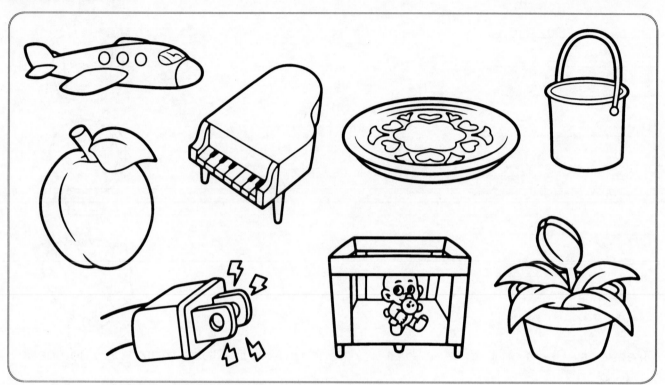

**Directions:** Add **pl** to the beginning of each group of letters. Trace and read the words you made. Listen for the **beginning pl blend**.

_____ ay

_____ us

_____ ace

_____ ow

_____ ease

**Directions:** Draw a plant in the pot. Color your picture.

Name: _____

# Beginning Sl Blends

**Directions:** Add **sl** to the beginning of each group of letters. Trace and read each word and then draw a line to the correct item.

_____ ed

_____ eeve

_____ ide

_____ ipper

_____ ice

_____ eep

Name: _____

# L Blends Review

**Directions:** Listen to the beginning blend for each item. Fill in the correct circle for each beginning blend.

①   (bl) (cl) (fl) (gl) (pl) (sl)

② 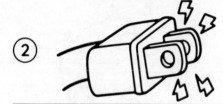 (bl) (cl) (fl) (gl) (pl) (sl)

③  (bl) (cl) (fl) (gl) (pl) (sl)

④ 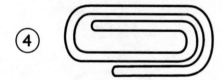 (bl) (cl) (fl) (gl) (pl) (sl)

⑤  (bl) (cl) (fl) (gl) (pl) (sl)

⑥  (bl) (cl) (fl) (gl) (pl) (sl)

⑦  (bl) (cl) (fl) (gl) (pl) (sl)

Name: _____

# Beginning Br Blends

**Directions:** Add **br** to the beginning of each group of letters. Reach each word and listen to the **br blend**. Trace each word. Then, draw a line to the correct item.

_____ush

_____anch

_____ead

_____ick

_____oom

_____ain

*#9102 Learning to Read Using Phonics*

Name: _____

# Beginning Cr Blends

**Directions:** Add **cr** to the beginning of each group of letters. Read each word and listen to the **cr blend**. Trace each word.

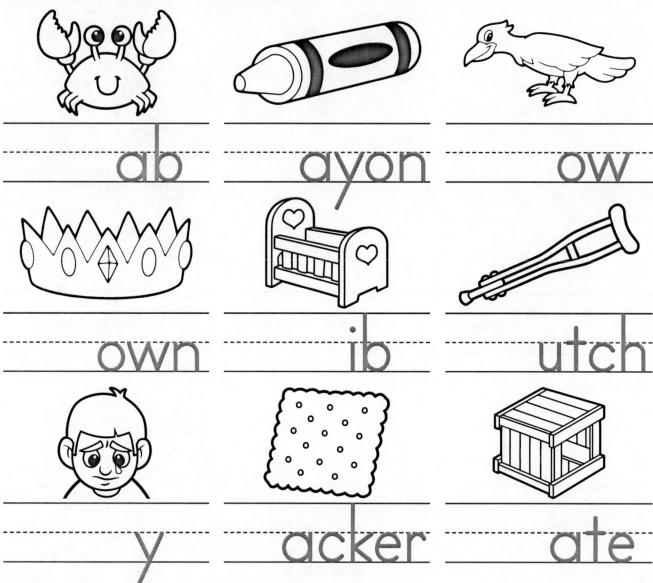

ab     ayon     ow

own     ib     utch

y     acker     ate

**Directions:** Sound out the **cr blend** word and trace it. Then, color the picture.

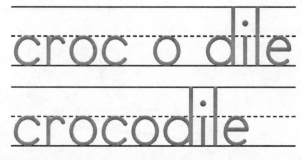

croc o dile

crocodile

Name: _____

# Beginning Dr Blends

**Directions:** Add **dr** to the beginning of each group of letters. Read each word and listen to the **dr blend**. Trace each word.

eam            ess            ____ink

agon            ip            um

**Directions:** Use the **dr** words in the word bank to fill in the blanks. Read each sentence.

( draw    drag    drive )

1. She can _____ many things.

2. Dad likes to _____ his car.

3. Please, _____ the desk here.

Name: _____

# Beginning Fr Blends

**Directions:** Name each item. Circle the items that begin with the **fr blend**. Cross out the other items.

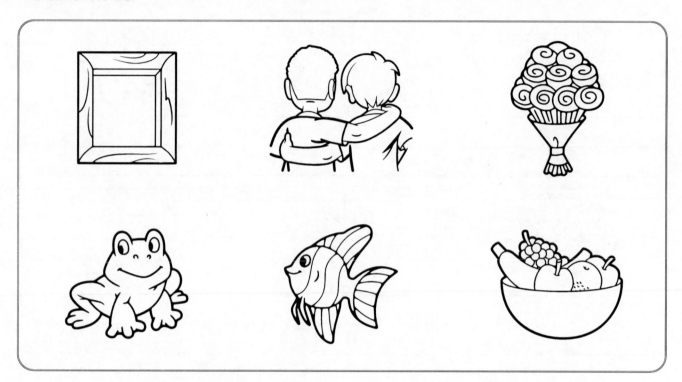

**Directions:** Use the **fr** words in the word bank to complete each sentence.

Friday    frown    front    free

1. If you do not have to pay, it is _____.

2. When you are mad, you _____.

3. _____ is a day of the week.

4. If you are first in line, you are in _____.

Name: _____

# Beginning Gr Blends

**Directions:** Read each sentence and circle the words that have **gr blends**. Use the directions at the top of each box to finish each picture.

**Directions:** Draw **gr**ass. Use a **gr**een crayon.

The green grass looks good!

**Directions:** Add more **gr**een **gr**apes to the vine.

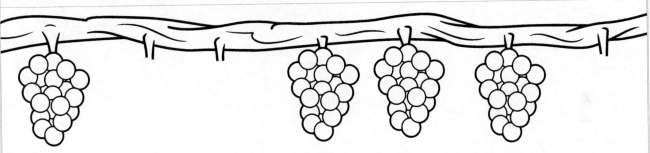

Green grapes grow on a vine.

**Directions:** Draw your picture with a **gr**in.

I have a great big grin.

**Directions:** Add your **gr**ade number.

I am in grade

_____.

Name: _____

# Beginning Tr Blends

**Directions:** Add **tr** to the beginning of each group of letters. Read the words and listen to the **tr blend**. Trace each word. Circle the **tr blend** words that you can ride.

ain          ee          ike

out          uck          actor

**Directions:** **Tr**ace the sentence and color the **tr**oll.

I see a troll!

Name: _____

# R Blends Review

**Directions:** Listen to the beginning blend for each item.  Fill in the circle with the correct letters for each beginning blend.

 ①   br  dr  fr  gr  tr

②   br  cr  fr  gr  tr

③   br  dr  fr  gr  tr

④   br  cr  fr  gr  tr

⑤   br  cr  fr  gr  tr

⑥   br  dr  fr  gr  tr

⑦   br  cr  fr  gr  tr

Name: _____

# Beginning Sc and Sk Blends

## Sc Blends

**Directions:** Add **sc** to the beginning of each group of letters. Trace and read each word.

____ ale     ____ ooter     ____ arf

A _____

____ arecrow

____ ares birds.

## Sk Blends

**Directions:** Add **sk** to the beginning of each group of letters. Trace and read each word.

____ ate     ____ i     ____ irt

The ____ unk rides
the ____ ateboard.

Name: _____

# Beginning Sm and Sn Blends

**Directions:** Look at each picture and the letter clues. Add **sm** or **sn** to the beginning to complete the word. Trace and read each word.

_____ile          _____ail          _____ock

_____ell          _____ake          _____oke

**Directions:** Add **sm**oke coming out of the chimney. Draw a **sn**owman in the **sn**ow.

Name: _____

# Beginning Sp Blends

**Directions:** Add **sp** to the beginning of each group of letters. Read and trace each word. Clap the syllables for each **sp** word.

_____ ider      _____ inner      _____ oon

_____ out      _____ ill      _____ ot

**Directions:** Read each sentence and trace the **sp** words. Answer each question.

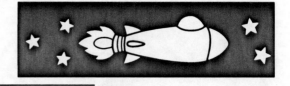

Would you like to go into space?    Yes    No

Do you like spaghetti?    Yes    No

Name: _____

# Beginning St Blends

**Directions:** Add **st** to the beginning of each group of letters. Trace and read the word.
Listen for the **st blend**. Draw a line to match each word to its picture.

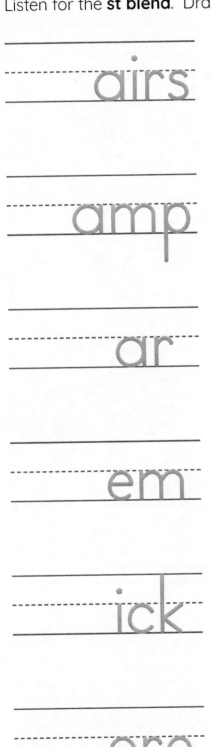

_____airs

_____amp

_____ar

_____em

_____ick

_____ore

Name: _____

# Beginning Sw Blends

**Directions:** Name each item. Circle the items that begin with the **sw blend**. Cross out the other items.

**Directions:** Add **sw** to the beginning of each group of letters. Trace and read each word.

| | | |
|---|---|---|
| _____ im | _____ an | _____ eet |
| _____ eep | _____ ing | _____ itch |

Name: _____

# S Blends Review

**Directions:** Name each item and listen to the beginning sound. Fill in the circle with the correct blend.

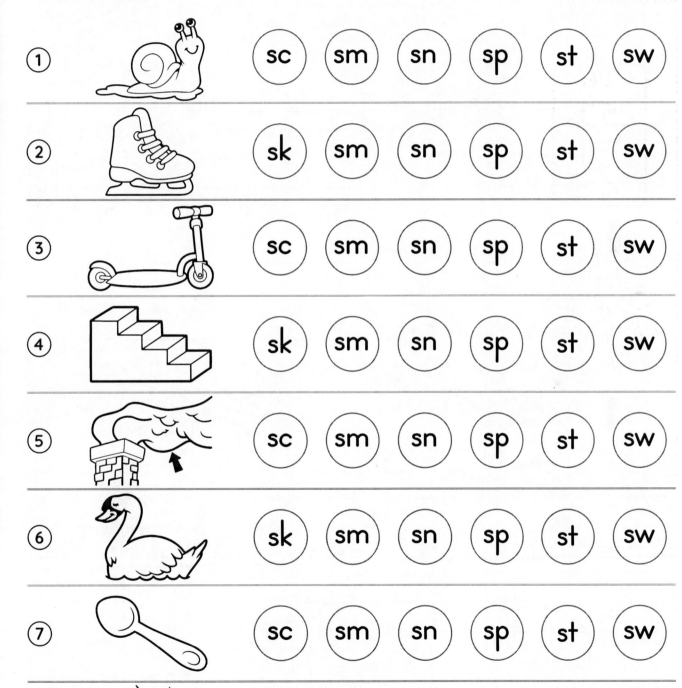

1  sc  sm  sn  sp  st  sw

2  sk  sm  sn  sp  st  sw

3  sc  sm  sn  sp  st  sw

4  sk  sm  sn  sp  st  sw

5  sc  sm  sn  sp  st  sw

6  sk  sm  sn  sp  st  sw

7  sc  sm  sn  sp  st  sw

8  sk  sm  sn  sp  st  sw

Name: _____

# Ends with -ft

**Directions:** Read the **ft** words in the word bank. Use the words to complete the sentences.

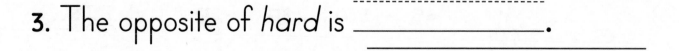

gift   left   soft   swift

1. He writes with his _____ hand.

2. She got a birthday _____.

3. The opposite of *hard* is _____.

4. Another word for *fast* is _____.

**Directions:** Read and trace the sentences. Circle the words with an **ft** ending.

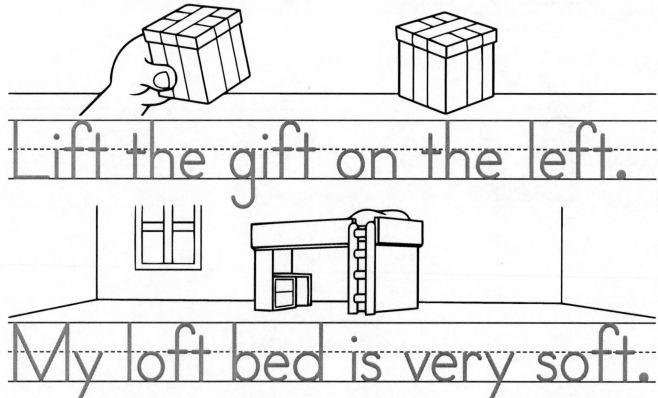

Lift the gift on the left.

My loft bed is very soft.

Name: _____

# Ends with -mp

**Directions:** Name each item and read each **mp** word in the box. Circle the correct word with an **mp ending** for each picture.

blimp    chimp

ramp    lamp

bump    pump

stamp    stump

champ    camp

ramp    damp

**Directions:** Read and trace the sentences. Circle the words ending with the **mp blend**.

We camp in a swamp.

I jump off the stump.

Name: _____

# Ends with -nd

**Directions:** Use the word wheels to write rhyming words that end with the **nd blend**.

| ba  ha | be  me | fi  mi |
|--------|--------|--------|
| sa **nd** la | le **nd** te | ki **nd** hi |
| sta | se | wi |

_____    _____    _____

---------------------------    ---------------------------    ---------------------------

_____    _____    _____

---------------------------    ---------------------------    ---------------------------

_____    _____    _____

---------------------------    ---------------------------    ---------------------------

_____    _____    _____

---------------------------    ---------------------------    ---------------------------

_____    _____    _____

---------------------------    ---------------------------    ---------------------------

Name: _____

# Ends with -nk

**Directions:** Add **nk** to the end of each group of letters. Trace and read each word.

tru___

si___

ta___

wi___

ba___

sa___

**Directions:** Read and trace the sentences. Circle the words ending with the **nk blend**.

Did the skunk stink?

The pink pig said, "Oink!"

Name: _____

# Ends with -nt

**Directions:** Add **nt** to the end of each group of letters. Trace and read each word that ends with the **nt blend**. Then, draw a line to its picture.

a _____

ce _____

pai _____

te _____

pla _____

**Directions:** Use the word wheel to write rhyming words that end with the **nt blend**.

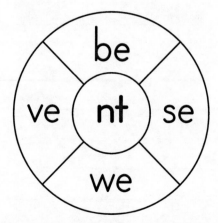

_____  _____

_____  _____

_____  _____

74

Name: _____

# Ends with -sk

**Directions:** Read and trace the sentence. Circle the word with an **sk ending**. Add snakes to the rock and finish the picture.

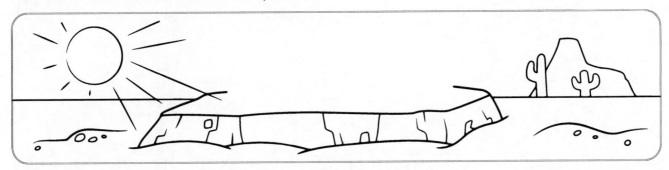

Snakes bask on rocks.

**Directions:** Name each item and read each **sk** word in the box. Circle the correct word ending with an **sk blend** for each picture.

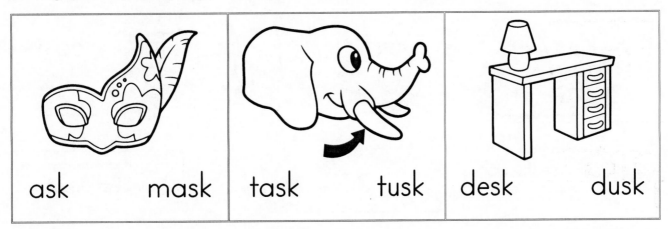

ask    mask    |    task    tusk    |    desk    dusk

**Directions:** Write **sk** after each set of letters to complete each word. In each row, cross out the word ending with an **sk blend** that does not rhyme.

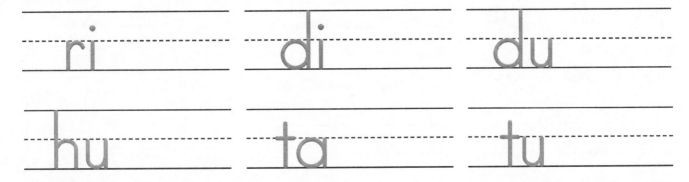

ri____     di____     du____

hu____     ta____     tu____

Name: _____

# Ends with -st

**Directions:** Read the words in each box ending with the **st blend**. Circle the correct word for each picture.

first    fist

must    dust

last    list

best

rest

nest

past

cast

vast

**Directions:** Use the word wheel to make **st** words.

ca

fa    st    la

pa

_____

_____

_____

_____

_____

Draw your be**st** gho**st**.

Name: _____

# Ending Blends Review

**Directions:** Name each item and listen to the ending sound. Fill in the circle with the correct letters for each ending blend.

①   ( ft )  ( mp )  ( nd )  ( nk )  ( nt )  ( sk )

②   ( mp )  ( nd )  ( nk )  ( nt )  ( sk )  ( st )

③   ( ft )  ( mp )  ( nd )  ( nk )  ( nt )  ( sk )

④   ( mp )  ( nd )  ( nk )  ( nt )  ( sk )  ( st )

⑤   ( ft )  ( mp )  ( nd )  ( nk )  ( nt )  ( sk )

⑥   ( mp )  ( nd )  ( nk )  ( nt )  ( sk )  ( st )

⑦   ( ft )  ( mp )  ( nd )  ( nk )  ( nt )  ( sk )

⑧   ( mp )  ( nd )  ( nk )  ( nt )  ( sk )  ( st )

Name: _____

# Beginning Ch Digraph

**Directions:** Add **ch** to the beginning of each group of letters. Trace and read each word. What is the sound **ch** makes?

___ ain          ___ eese          ___ air

___ erry          ___ ick          ___ in

**Directions:** Read and trace each sentence. Circle the **ch** words.

That chick can chirp!

We like chips and chili.

Name: _____

# Beginning Sh Digraph

**Directions:** Add **sh** to the beginning of each group of letters. Trace and read each word. Listen for the **sh sound**.

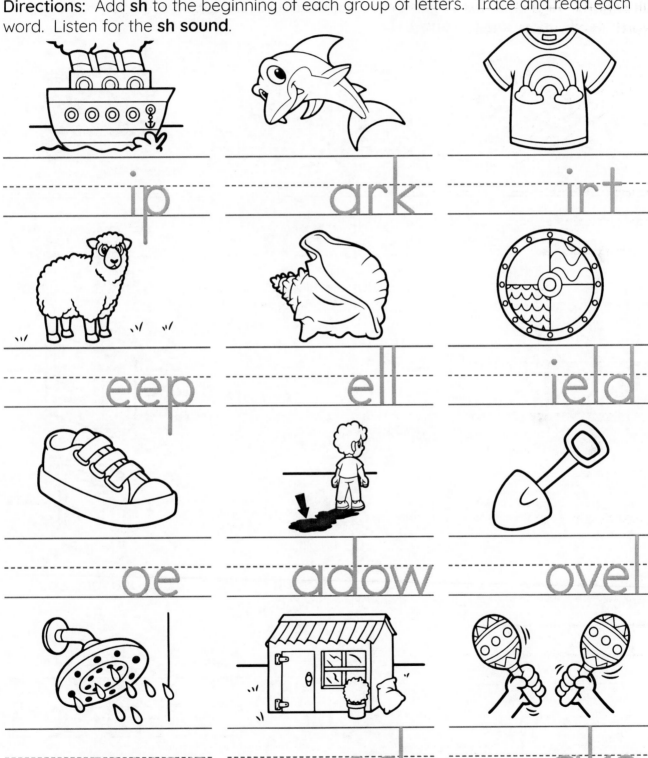

ip

ark

irt

eep

ell

ield

oe

adow

ovel

ower

ed

ake

Name: _____

# Beginning Th Digraph

**Directions:** Add **th** to the beginning of each group of letters. Trace and read each word and listen for the **th sound**.

_____ orn          _____ ink          _____ umb

**Directions:** Read and trace the two words below. Draw lines to match the words to the books you see. Which one is *thick* and which one is *thin*?

thick

thin

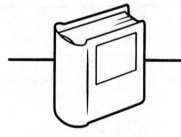

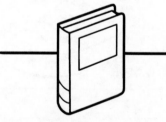

**Directions:** Add **th** to the beginning of each group of letters. Trace and read each number word and draw a line to the correct number.

_____ ree

_____ irty

13

30

3

_____ irteen

Name: _____

# Beginning Wh Digraph

**Directions:** Add **wh** to the beginning of each group of letters. Trace and read each word and draw a line to its picture. Listen to the **wh sound**.

_____ istle

_____ ale

_____ eel

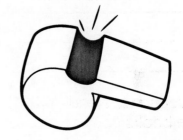

**Directions:** Add **wh** to the beginning of each group of letters. Trace and read each question word.

_____ at

_____ ere

_____ en

_____ y

_____ ich

Name: _____

# Beginning Digraph Review

**Directions:** Name the items in each row. Circle the items in each row that have the correct beginning sound. Cross out the item that does not have the correct sound.

**Directions:** Write the correct beginning letters for each item. Use **ch**, **sh**, **th**, or **wh**.

___eat     ___ip     ___umb     ___air

Name: _____

# Ending Digraph -ch

**Directions:** Add **ch** to the end of each group of letters. Trace and read each word.

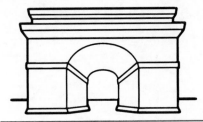  

ar _____   bea _____   pea _____

roa _____   coa _____   cou _____

**Directions:** Use the words with **ch endings** in the word bank to complete each sentence.

| each | much | rich | teach |
| --- | --- | --- | --- |

1. Give _____ child a pen.

2. I will _____ the dog a trick.

3. How _____ time do you need?

4. The king is very _____.

Name: _____

# Ending Digraph -ck

**Directions:** When **ck** comes at the end of a word it follows a short vowel. Use the word wheels to make rhyming words that end in **ck**. Read each group of words.

ba | cra
sa | **ck** | ha
tra

du | clu
lu | **ck** | pu
tru

lo | do
ro | **ck** | so
clo

_____
- - - - - - - - - - -
_____
- - - - - - - - - - -
_____
- - - - - - - - - - -
_____
- - - - - - - - - - -
_____
- - - - - - - - - - -
_____
- - - - - - - - - - -
_____

Name: _____

# Ending Digraph -sh

**Directions:** Read the words with **sh endings** in each box. Circle the correct word for each item.

| dish    fish | blush    brush | wish    wash |
| cash    crash | rush    hush | bush    push |

**Directions:** Add **sh** to the end of each group of letters. Trace and read the words.

da_____          sma_____

ma_____          tra_____

ra_____          fla_____

Name: _____

# Ending Digraph -th

**Directions:** Add **th** to the end of each group of letters. Trace and read the words and then draw lines to the correct items.

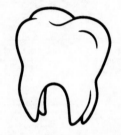

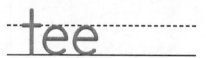

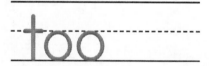

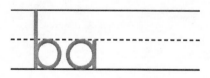

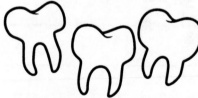

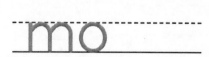

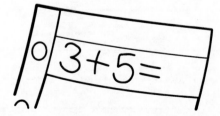

Name: _____

# Ending Digraph Review

**Directions:** Name each item and listen to the ending sound. Fill in the circle that has the correct ending.

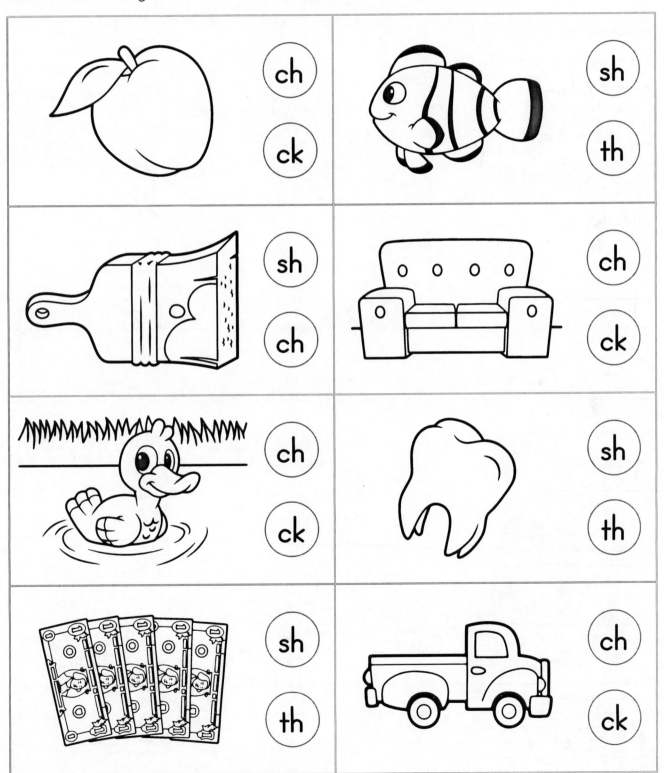

Name: _____

# Ending Trigraphs -nch and -tch

## nch

**Directions:** Add the **nch ending** to complete the words in each row. Trace and read the words you made.

 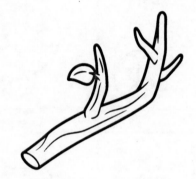 

be_____     bra_____     wre_____

## tch

**Directions:** Add the **tch ending** to complete the words in each row. Trace and read the words you made.

  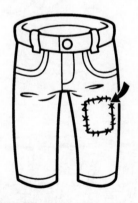

wa_____     ha_____     pa_____

Name: _____

# More -nch and -tch Words

**Directions:** Use the word wheels to make more **nch** and **tch** words. Read each group of rhyming words.

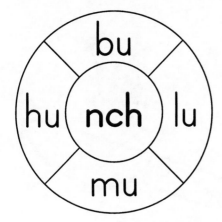

_____  _____

- - - - - - - - - - - -  - - - - - - - - - - - -

_____  _____

- - - - - - - - - - - -  - - - - - - - - - - - -

_____  _____

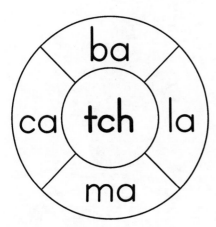

_____  _____

- - - - - - - - - - - -  - - - - - - - - - - - -

_____  _____

- - - - - - - - - - - -  - - - - - - - - - - - -

_____  _____

**Directions:** Circle the best word with an **nch** or **tch ending** to complete each sentence. Cross out the other word. Read the completed sentence.

He grew an    inch    taller.
       itch

My bug bite makes me    inch    .
             itch

Name: _____

# Silent K

**Directions:** Add **kn** to the beginning of each group of letters.  The **k** will be silent in each word.  Trace and read the words and then draw lines to the correct items.

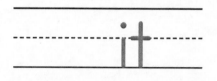 it

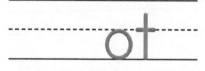 ee

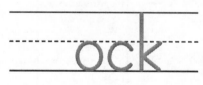 ot

 ight

 ock

ife

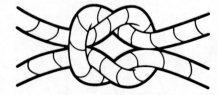

Did you **kn**ow each word would sound like it starts with the letter **n**?

# Silent W

**Directions:** Add **wr** to the beginning of each group of letters. Trace and read the words. The **w** is silent. The words will sound like they start with **r**.

_____eath    _____en    _____ist

**Directions:** Add **wr** to the beginning of each group of letters. Read and trace the *action words*. The **w** is silent. The words will sound like they start with **r**.

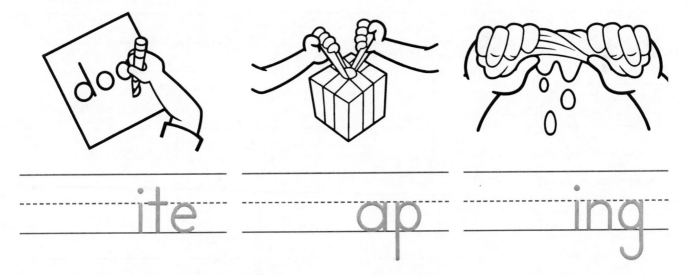

_____ite    _____ap    _____ing

**Directions:** Choose the correct **wr** word to complete the sentence. Read the sentence.

| wreath    wring    write |
|---|

Use your wrists to _____ out the cloth.

       #9102 *Learning to Read Using Phonics*

Name: _____

# Long Vowel Team -ai

**Directions:** Sometimes, when two vowels walk together, the first one does the talking. Add **ai** to complete the **long a** words in each word family. Trace and read the words.

### ail Family

m___    n___    p___

s___    t___    tr___

### ain Family

m___    p___    r___

st___n    br___n    ch___n

**Directions:** Read and trace the sentence. Circle the **ai** words.

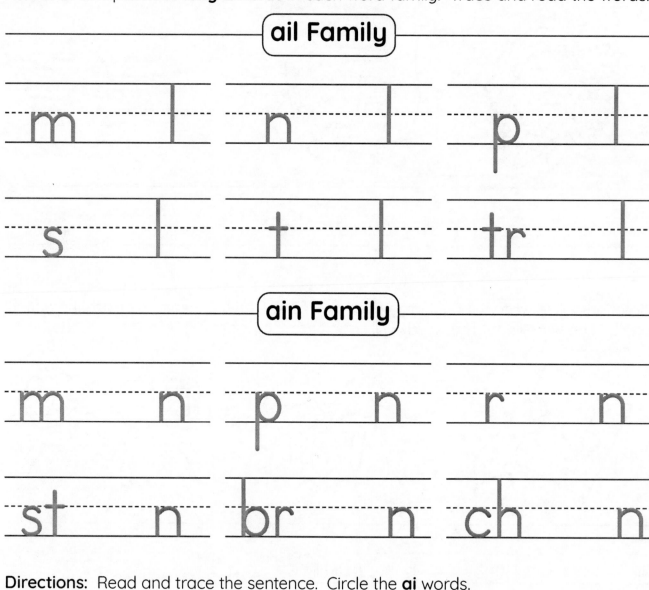

Quail and snail are on

the train.

Name: _____

# Long Vowel Team -ay

**Directions:** The **ay vowel team** makes the **long a** sound. Use the word wheel to make **ay** words. Read the rhyming words.

_____    _____
_____    _____
_____    _____
_____    _____
_____    _____

**Directions:** Choose a word from the **ay** family to complete each sentence. Read each sentence. Circle all the **ay** words. Did you find 10?

| Today    play    pay    tray |

1. We play with clay on the _____.

2. _____ is my birthday!

3. We will _____ for the hay.

4. Jay will stay to _____ cards.

Name: _____

# Long Vowel Team -ea

**Directions:** Add **ea** to complete the words in each word family. Read each word and listen to the **long e** sound. Circle the word in each box that matches the picture.

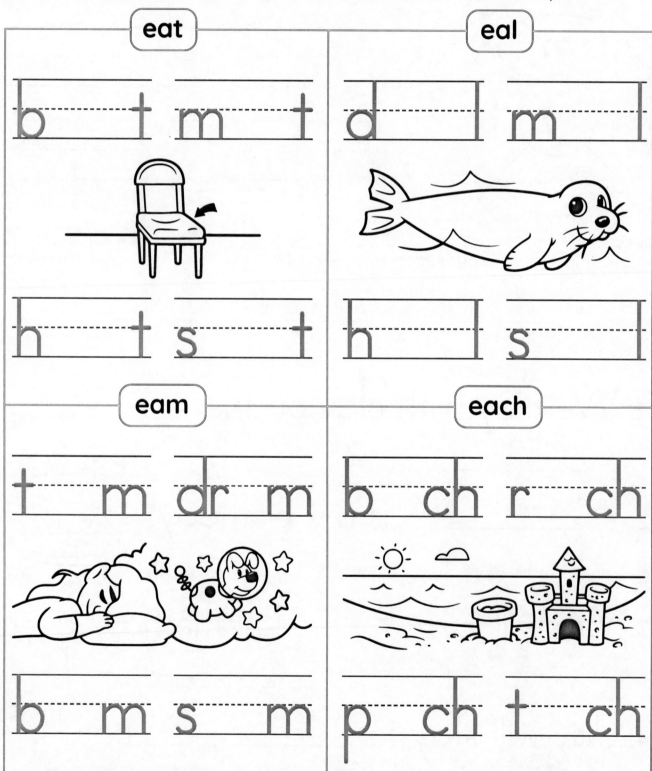

Name: _____

# Long Vowel Team -ee

**Directions:** Sort the words in the word bank. Put the **ee** words in the correct word family columns. Then read the words in each family.

| cheek | deep | feed | keep | need | peek |
| seed | seek | sleep | sweep | weed | week |

## eep

## eed

## eek

## Can you think of more words for each family?

Name: _____

# Long Vowel Team -ie

**Directions:** The **ie vowel team** can make the **long i** sound. Add **ie** to the letters below. Trace and read each word. Listen for the **long i** sound.

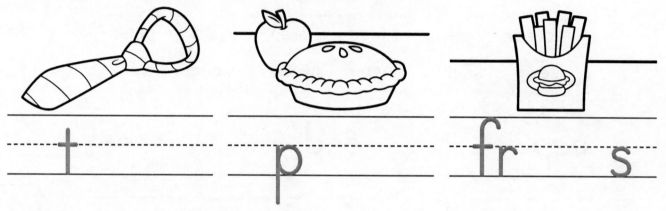

t _____     p _____     fr _____    s _____

**Directions:** Read each sentence. Circle the correct **ie** word at the end to complete each sentence. Write the word on the lines.

**1.** It is not nice to tell a _____.

> lie
> tie

**2.** The baby _____ if she is hungry.

> cries
> flies

**3.** I do not want the old tree to _____.

> pie
> die

Name: _____

# Long Vowel Team -oa

**Directions:** The **oa vowel team** makes the **long o** sound. Add **oa** to complete the words below. Trace and read each word.

b _ _ t     r _ _ d     g _ _ t

c _ _ t     s _ _ p     t _ _ st

**Directions:** Read the **oa** words in the word bank to fill in the blanks. Read each sentence.

( float    moat    toad )

**1.** My brother just got a pet _____.

**2.** She will _____ in the pool in her new tube.

**3.** The water around a castle is called a _____.

Name: _____

# Long Vowel Teams -ue and -ui

## ue

**Directions:** The **ue** vowel team makes the **long u** sound. Use the word wheel to make some **ue** words. Read the rhyming words.

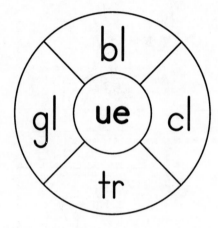

bl
gl   ue   cl
tr

_____          _____
- - - - - - - - - - - - - - -          - - - - - - - - - - - - - - -
_____          _____
- - - - - - - - - - - - - - -          - - - - - - - - - - - - - - -
_____          _____

## ui

**Directions:** Read the **ui** words in the word bank. Each **ui** word makes the **long u** sound. Use the words in the word bank to finish the story below.

> fruit    suit    ruin    juice

_____
- - - - - - - - - - -

1. I spilled a box of _____.

_____
- - - - - - - - - - -

2. It was _____ juice.

_____
- - - - - - - - - - - !

3. It is all over my _____!

_____
- - - - - - - - - - -

4. I hope I did not _____ it.

Name: _____

# Long Vowel Teams Review

**Directions:** Circle the correct word to complete each sentence. Write each word on the line. Read each sentence to check your answers.

| | |
|---|---|
| **1** I got a _____ on my shirt. | stain train |
| **2** Our dog has a little _____. | sail tail |
| **3** Will you _____ with us today? | tray play |
| **4** We will fix my toy with _____. | clue glue |
| **5** The old _____ was green. | jeep beep |
| **6** There is a _____ on the road. | moat goat |
| **7** Mom will _____ up her tea. | meat heat |

# The -aw Sound

**Directions:** Add **aw** to the end of each consonant. Trace and read the **aw** words. What sound does **aw** make?

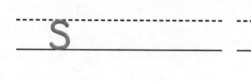
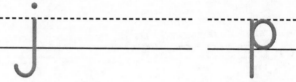

s     j     p

**Directions:** Add **aw** to the end of each blend. Read the **aw** words.

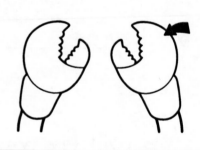

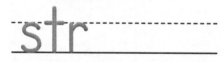
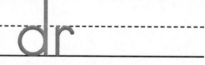

str     dr     cl

**Directions:** Add **aw** to the middle of each word. Read the **aw** words.

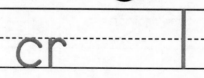

f   n     cr     h   k

Name: _____

# The -ew Sound

**Directions:** Add **ew** to the end of each consonant. Trace and read the **ew** words. Do they sound like **long u** words?

n _____ f _____ m _____ d _____

**Directions:** Circle the correct **ew** word in the box to complete each sentence. Write the word on the lines. Read each sentence.

| 1 | Belle _____ out the candles! | blew brew |
|---|---|---|
| 2 | Spot likes to _____ on his bone. | drew chew |
| 3 | The baby birds _____ away. | flew grew |
| 4 | I need a _____ to fix the door. | knew screw |
| 5 | Tom made a yummy _____. | stew threw |

Name: _____

# The -oi Sound

**Directions:** Add **oi** to complete the words below. Read the words. The **oi vowel team** sounds like the beginning of the sound a little pig makes—*oink!*

b_____    c_____    s_____

c_____    n_____    dr_____ d_____    f_____

**Directions:** Add **oi** to complete each word. Read the words. Circle the two words in each row that rhyme.

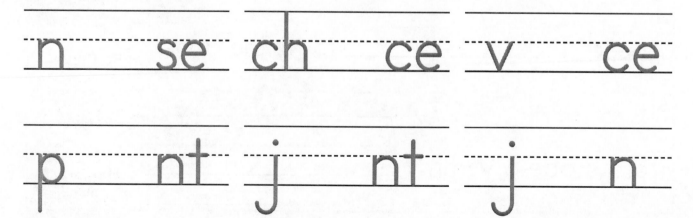

n_____    se____    ch____    ce____    v_____    ce____

p_____    ____nt    j_____    ____nt    j_____    ____n

Name: _____

# The -oo Sound in "Hook"

**Directions:** Add **oo** to the middle of each group of letters. Trace and read the **oo** words. Listen for the sound the **oo** makes in these words.

h __ k       c __ k       h __ f

c __ kie       h __ d       die

**Directions:** Write the correct **oo** word to complete each sentence. Read the sentences. Circle the other words in the sentences that have the same **oo** sounds.

| book | foot | hood | wood |

**1.** She took a _____ to the nook.

**2.** She shook the grass off her _____.

**3.** He got good _____ for the fire.

**4.** He stood to look under the _____.

Name: _____

# The -oo Sound in "Hoop"

**Directions:** Name the items in the column on the left. Then trace the **oo** words on the right. Draw lines to match each picture to a word that rhymes with it. One has been done for you.

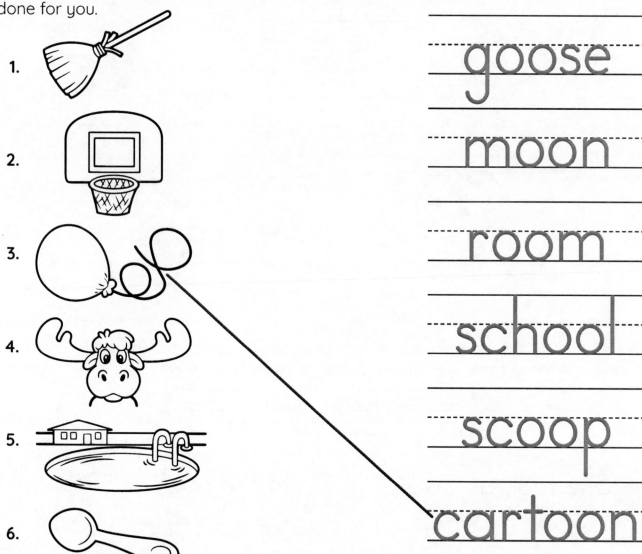

1.

2.

3.

4.

5.

6.

goose

moon

room

school

scoop

cartoon

**Directions:** Use **oo** words to answer the questions below.

7. What does a ghost say? _____

8. What does a cow say? _____

Name: _____

# When -ou Sounds Like "Oww"

**Directions:** Add **ou** to the middle of each group of letters. Trace and read the **ou vowel team** words. Circle the two words that rhyme. Do you hear how the **o** and **u** glide together?

c l          c ch          h se

m se          sp t          m th

**Directions:** Read the **ou vowel team** words in the stars. Find three sets of words that rhyme. Color each set of words that rhyme. Use a different color for each set.

about          cloud          found          loud          out

proud          round          shout          sound

Name: _____

# The -ow Sound

**Directions:** Sometimes **ow** sounds like the **ow** in **cow**.  Read the **ow** words in each row. Circle the word that matches the picture at the beginning.

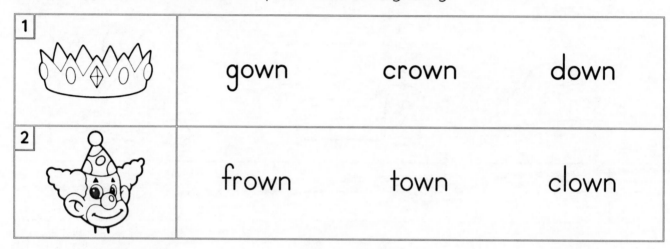

| 1 | | gown | crown | down |
|---|---|------|-------|------|
| 2 | | frown | town | clown |

**Directions:** Add **ow** to complete each two-syllable word.  Trace and read the words.

fl___ er

t___ el

t___ er

___ me

sh___ er

Name: _____

# When -ow Sounds Like "Oh!"

**Directions:** Sometimes, **ow** makes the **long o** sound. Read each sentence. Circle the **ow** words that have the **ow** sound like "oh!"

**1.** He has a bow and arrow.

**2.** I know we can tow the car.

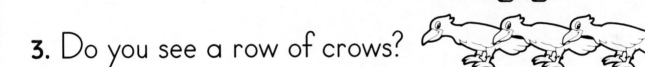

**3.** Do you see a row of crows?

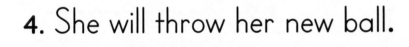

**4.** She will throw her new ball.

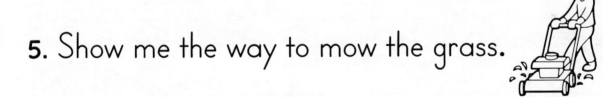

**5.** Show me the way to mow the grass.

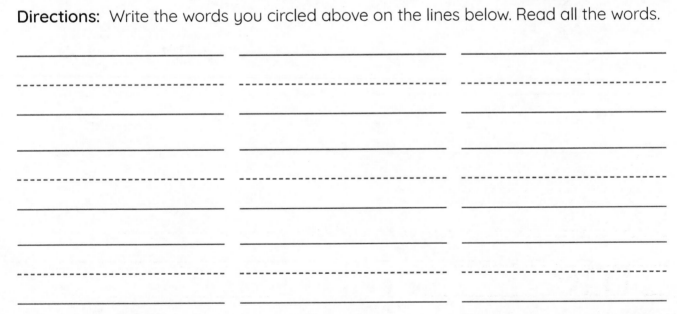

**Directions:** Write the words you circled above on the lines below. Read all the words.

_____  _____  _____

_____  _____  _____

_____  _____  _____

_____  _____  _____

_____  _____  _____

_____  _____  _____

Name: _____

# Vowel Sounds Review

**Directions:** Name the item in each box. Then, circle the correct letters to complete each word. Write the letters and read the word.

| | |
|---|---|
| aw<br>ew<br><br>_____<br>str | oo<br>oi<br><br>b____l |
| oo<br>ou<br><br>c____d | aw<br>ew<br><br>_____<br>scr |

**Directions:** Sort the words in the word bank by listening to the **oo vowel team** sound each word makes. Write the words in the correct column.

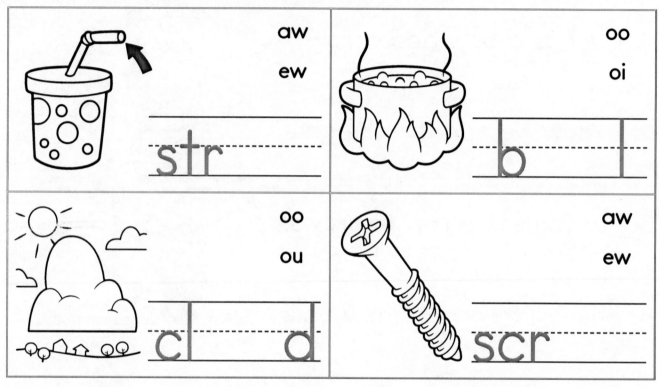

| foot | boot | soon | wood |

| oo like "hoop" | oo like "hook" |
|---|---|
| _____ | _____ |
| _____ | _____ |
| _____ | _____ |
| _____ | _____ |
| _____ | _____ |

# Answer Key

**Page 6**
b: Draw lines to the *balloon* and the *bone*.
d: Draw lines to the *drum* and the *door*.
j: Draw lines to the *jam* and the *jar*.
p: Draw lines to the *pancakes* and the *pizza*.
q: Draw lines to the *quilt* and the *quail*.
y: Draw lines to the *yo-yo* and the *yarn*.

**Page 7**
Row 1: cart, gum, top
Row 2: zip, van, bun
Row 3: feet, hive, goat
Row 4: lion, bunny, milk

**Page 8**
Row 1: Circle the *s* for sun, *f* for fan, and *h* for hand.
Row 2: Circle the *b* for bike, *k* for kite, and *g* for gate.
Row 3: Circle the *l* for lamp, *r* for ring, and *w* for wagon.
Check for three words beginning with **d**.

**Page 9**
Row 1: bug, pig, nut
Row 2: wig, mug, hut
*bug* rhymes with *mug*
*pig* rhymes with *wig*
*nut* rhymes with *hut*

**Page 10**
Row 1: Circle the *yarn* and the *yo-yo*.
    Cross out the *train*.
    Circle the *volcano* and the *vacuum*. Cross out the *pin*.
Row 2: Circle the *juice* and the *jar*.
    Cross out the *kite*.
    Circle the *fish* and the *fork*.
    Cross out the *lamp*.
Row 3: Circle the *horse* and the *hose*.
    Cross out the *wagon*.
    Circle the *saw* and the *sun*.
    Cross out the *nest*.
Row 4: Circle the *game* and the *glue*.
    Cross out the *cupcake/cake*.
    Circle the *moon* and the *milk*.
    Cross out the *car*.

**Page 11**
Draw a line to match *pie* and *pizza*.
Draw a line to match *zipper* and *zebra*.
Draw a line to match *rake* and *rabbit*.
Draw a line to match *car* and *cat*.
Draw a line to match *gate* and *goat*.
Draw a line to match *quilt* and *quail*.
Draw a line to match *dog* and *dragon*.

**Page 12**
Circle: castle, cube, car
Sentence 1: Circle *cat* and *cot*.
Sentence 2: Circle *corn* and *cob*.
Sentence 3: Circle *Cole* and *cast*.
cactus-2          coconut-3

**Page 13**
Soft C: cent, dice, mice, fence, city, pencil
Hard C: comb, cart, cabin
The first *c* in *bicycle* is soft. The second *c* is hard.

**Page 14**
Circle: glue, goat, grill
Cross out: gem
Sentence 1: Circle *girl, gave,* and *gift*.
Sentence 2: Circle *go, get,* and *gas*.
Sentence 3: Circle *grew, green,* and *grapes*.
guitar-2          gorilla-3

**Page 15**
Check for understanding of *germs* and *gems*.
Circle: huge, giraffe, gentle, giant
The first *g* in *gigantic* is soft and the second *g* is hard.

**Page 16**
Row 1: Circle the *d* for hand, *g* for flag, and *l* for ball.
Row 2: Circle the *m* for drum, *s* for bus, and *f* for scarf.
Ending consonants: tu**b**, be**d**, ru**g**

**Page 17**
p: Draw lines to the *soap* and the *ship*.
r: Draw lines to the *ear* and the *star*.
s: Draw lines to the *dress* and the *gas*.
t: Draw lines to the *boot* and the *nest*.
x: Draw lines to the *ax* and the *box*.

**Page 18**
Row 1: mug, four, soap
Row 2: camel, six, vacuum
Row 3: crab, seven, crib
Row 4: bird, ten, elf

**Page 19**
Row 1: **t**en**t**, **k**ic**k**
Row 2: **b**ul**b**, **p**um**p**
lion-roar
12 o'clock-noon
chick-peep

**Page 20**
1. off
2. stiff
3. sniff
4. cliff and bluff
5. *waffle* and *muffin*

**Page 21**
Check that all four words are written for each word wheel.
ll: ball, bill, bull, bell
ll: fall, fill, full, fell
*balloon* and *pillow*

**Page 22**
Row 1: grass, dress, kiss
Row 2: toss, chess, floss
1. recess
2. mess
3. pass

**Page 23**
Top boxes: Check that lines are drawn correctly.
Row 1: button, rattle, mitten
Row 2: kitten, bottle, butter

**Page 24**
Adding zz: buzz, jazz, fizz
1. pizza
2. fuzzy
3. fizzy
4. frizzy
5. puzzle

**Page 25**
1. Underline <u>kitten</u> and <u>cliff</u>.
2. Underline <u>yellow</u> and <u>puffy</u>.
3. Underline <u>toss</u>, <u>ball</u>, and <u>grass</u>.
4. Underline <u>little</u> and <u>muffins</u>.
5. Underline <u>press</u>, <u>all</u>, and <u>buttons</u>.
ff: cliff, puffy, muffins
ll: yellow, ball, all
ss: toss, grass, press
tt: kitten, little, buttons

**Page 26**
The c<u>a</u>t h<u>a</u>s a h<u>a</u>t.
It is a p<u>a</u>n!
I have a p<u>e</u>t h<u>e</u>n.
Its n<u>e</u>st is on a sl<u>e</u>d.
Row 1: net, gas
Row 2: bat, ten

**Page 27**
The p<u>i</u>g has a b<u>i</u>g b<u>i</u>b.
The d<u>o</u>g g<u>o</u>t a m<u>o</u>p.
*b<u>u</u>g* rhymes with *r<u>u</u>g*
*s<u>u</u>b* rhymes with *t<u>u</u>b*
*s<u>u</u>n* rhymes with *b<u>u</u>n*

**Page 28**
Row 1: box, nut, bat
Row 2: web, gum, lip
Row 3: fan, pig, dog
Row 4: frog, nest, fish

**Page 29**
1. net
2. map
3. pup
4. pig
5. log
6. rug

**Page 30**
Row 1: cart, far, barn
Row 2: hard, part, jar
*cart* and *part* rhyme; *far* and *jar* rhyme
1. shark, card
2. park, car
3. stars, dark
4. are, farm

**Page 31**
1. Her, fern, water
2. tower, river
Row 1: taller, slower
Row 2: shorter, faster
Adding *er* to these words turns them into comparing words

**Page 32**
Row 1: shirt, fir, bird
Row 2: stir, dirt, stair
*dirt* and *shirt* rhyme; *fir* and *stir* rhyme; *hair* and *stair* rhyme
1. bird, chirp
2. twirl, skirt
3. first, third
4. dirt, shirt

**Page 33**
corn
fort
fork
stork
door
cork
Check that lines have been drawn to the correct item for each word.

**Page 34**
Column 1: turkey, turtle
Column 2: church, nurse
Column 3: purse, spur
*blur* rhymes with *spur*; *four* rhymes with *your*; *hour* rhymes with *sour*

**Page 35**
Check that pairs of letters were circled in each row.
Row 1: bird, worm, arm
Row 2: door, fern, star
Row 3: barn, fort, river
Row 4: purse, girl, finger

**Page 36**
Row 1: cane, cape
Row 2: cube, kite
Row 3: mane, pine
Row 4: tape, tube

**Page 37**
Row 1: slide, gate, rake, game
Row 2: ate, bite, cute
Row 3: dime, fine, hope
Complete the word *cake*.

**Page 38**
Check that all four words are written for each word wheel.
**ake:** bake, fake, lake, cake
**ate:** date, late, mate, gate
**ace:** face, pace, race, lace

**Page 39**
Check that lines are drawn correctly from words to pictures.

**Page 40**
Color the ties with the following *long i* word pairs:
*dive* and *hive*
*pie* and *tie*
*dice* and *mice*
*time* and *dime*
*tire* and *fire*

**Page 41**
Listen as words are read to find rhyming words.
1. Cross out *robe*.
2. Cross out *rope*.
3. Cross out *soap*.
4. Cross out *blow*.

**Page 42**
1. mule
2. tube
3. flute
4. juice
5. glue
Underline the *e* at the end of each word: cut*e*, tun*e*, mut*e*.
Circle: *cute* and *mute*.

**Page 43**
Row 1: Circle *pose* and *rose*.
Row 2: Circle *mice* and *dice*.
Row 3: Circle *tube* and *cube*.
Row 4: Circle *bake* and *cake*.

**Page 44**
Check all six words from the word wheel: cry, dry, shy, why, try, fly
**Adding y:**
Row 1: bunny, lily, party
Row 2: curly, city, pony

**Page 45**
Row 1: by-**i**, happy-**e**
Row 2: penny-**e**, my-**i**
Row 3: fry-**i**, funny-**e**
Row 4: story-**e**, dirty-**e**
teddy-**e**, sky-**i**

**Page 46**
My puppy got all <u>muddy</u>!
Why is the tiny <u>kitty</u> so shy?
We saw the baby birds <u>try</u> to fly.
**Possible words for e ending sound:**
puppy, muddy, tiny, kitty, baby
**Possible words for i ending sound:**
My, Why, shy, try, fly

**Page 47**
Row 1: crayon, hotel, table
Row 2: music, paper, pilot
Row 3: tiger, ruler, spider
Row 4: arrow, robot, zero

**Page 48**
Row 1: *bell*-short, *comb*-long, *fire*-long
Row 2: *fish*-short, *flute*-long, *gas*-short
Row 3: *tree*-long, *game*-long, *tub*-short

**Page 49**
**Long Vowel Sound:** bike, bone, feet, cane
**Short Vowel Sound:** can, bed, sun, pig

**Page 50**
Circle: blimp, blanket, blocks, blow
**Cross out:** boots, ball
Row 1: blade, black, blog
Row 2: blend, blink, bloom
Circle: black

**Page 51**
Row 1: clam, clap, clip
Row 2: clean, cloud, cliff
Row 3: claw, clock, clay
Trace the word *clown* and finish the picture.

**Page 52**
Circle: flag, flower, fly, flute, and possibly "flake"
**Cross out:** fin, fan, feet, and possibly "snowflake"
Row 1: flame, floss, flip
Row 2: flat, flew, floor

**Page 53**
**Adding gl:** globe, gloves, glue
Check that lines are drawn correctly from words to pictures.
Check that lines are drawn correctly from *glass* and *glasses* to pictures.
**Adding gl:** glad, glide, glee
        *Glad* and *glee* mean happy.

**Page 54**
Circle: plane, plate, plum, plug, playpen, plant
**Cross out:** piano, pail
**Adding pl:** play, plus, place, plow, please

# Answer Key (cont.)

**Page 55**
**Adding sl:** sled, sleeve, slide, slipper, slice, sleep
Check that lines are drawn correctly from words to pictures.

**Page 56**
1. **sl** for sleep
2. **pl** for plug
3. **gl** for glasses
4. **cl** for clip
5. **fl** for flag
6. **sl** for slipper
7. **bl** for blocks

**Page 57**
**Adding br:** brush, branch, bread, brick, broom, brain
Check that lines are drawn correctly from words to pictures.

**Page 58**
**Row 1:** crab, crayon, crow
**Row 2:** crown, crib, crutch
**Row 3:** cry, cracker, crate

**Page 59**
**Row 1:** dream, dress, drink
**Row 2:** dragon, drip, drum
1. draw
2. drive
3. drag

**Page 60**
**Circle:** frame, friends, frog, fruit
**Cross out:** flowers, fish
1. free
2. frown
3. Friday
4. front

**Page 61**
Check the student work in each section.
**Circle:** green, grass
**Circle:** green, grapes, grow
**Circle:** great, grin
**Circle:** grade

**Page 62**
**Row 1:** train, tree, trike
**Row 2:** trout, truck, tractor
**Circle:** train, trike, truck, tractor

**Page 63**
1. **dr** for drum
2. **br** for broom
3. **fr** for frog
4. **gr** for grapes
5. **cr** for crown
6. **tr** for tractor
7. **cr** for crab

**Page 64**
**Adding sc:** scale, scooter, scarf, scarecrow, scares
**Adding sk:** skate, ski, skirt, skunk, skateboard

**Page 65**
**Row 1:** smile, snail, smock
**Row 2:** smell, snake, smoke
Check drawing for addition of *smoke* and a *snowman*.

**Page 66**
**Row 1:** spider, spinner, spoon
**Row 2:** spout, spill, spot
Discuss answers to questions.

**Page 67**
**Adding st:** stairs, stamp, star, stem, stick, store
Check that lines are drawn correctly from words to pictures.

**Page 68**
**Circle:** switch, swim, swing, swan, sweep, sweater
**Cross out:** sandwich, seesaw, star
**Row 1:** swim, swan, sweet
**Row 2:** sweep, swing, switch

**Page 69**
1. **sn** for snail
2. **sk** for skate
3. **sc** for scooter
4. **st** for stairs
5. **sm** for smoke
6. **sw** for swan
7. **sp** for spoon
8. **st** for star

**Page 70**
1. left
2. gift
3. soft
4. swift
**Circle:** lift, gift, left
**Circle:** loft, soft

**Page 71**
**Row 1:** blimp, lamp, pump
**Row 2:** stump, camp, ramp
**Sentence 1:** Circle *camp* and *swamp.*
**Sentence 2:** Circle *jump* and *stump.*

**Page 72**
**Column 1 Word Wheel:** hand, land, stand, sand, band
**Column 2 Word Wheel:** mend, tend, send, lend, bend
**Column 3 Word Wheel:** mind, hind, wind, kind, find

**Page 73**
**Row 1:** trunk, sink, tank
**Row 2:** wink, bank, sank
**Sentence 1:** Circle *skunk* and *stink.*
**Sentence 2:** Circle *pink* and *Oink.*

**Page 74**
ant
cent
paint
tent
plant
Check that lines are drawn correctly from words to pictures.
Check all four words from the word wheel: bent, sent, went, vent

**Page 75**
Circle the word *bask* and check for completion of the art.
**Circle:** mask, tusk, desk
**Row 1:** risk, disk, dusk—Cross out *dusk.*
**Row 2:** husk, task, tusk—Cross out *task.*

**Page 76**
**Row 1:** fist, dust, list
**Row 2:** nest, cast
Check that all four words are written from the word wheel: cast, last, past, fast

**Page 77**
1. **ft** for gift or **nt** for present.
2. **mp** for lamp
3. **nd** for hand
4. **nt** for tent
5. **mp** for blimp
6. **nk** for tank
7. **sk** for desk
8. **st** for fist or **nd** for hand.

**Page 78**
**Row 1:** chain, cheese, chair
**Row 2:** cherry, chick, chin
**Sentence 1:** Circle *chick* and *chirp.*
**Sentence 2:** Circle *chips* and *chili.*

**Page 79**
**Row 1:** ship, shark, shirt
**Row 2:** sheep, shell, shield
**Row 3:** shoe, shadow, shovel
**Row 4:** shower, shed, shake

**Page 80**
**Adding th:** thorn, think, thumb
Check that lines are drawn correctly to *thick* and *thin* books.
three—3
thirty—30
thirteen—13
Check that lines are drawn from words to correct numbers.

**Page 81**
**Adding wh:** whistle, whale, wheel
Check that lines are drawn from words to correct pictures.
**Question Words:** what, when, where, why, which

# Answer Key *(cont.)*

**Page 82**
**ch:** Circle *cherries, cheese,* and *chick.* Cross out *wheel.*
**sh:** Circle *shovel, shoe,* and *sheep.* Cross out *chain.*
**th:** Circle *thirteen, thorn,* and *thumb.* Cross out *shark/fish.*
**wh:** Circle *whistle, wheat, whale.* Cross out *chair.*
**Beginning Letters:** <u>wh</u>eat, <u>sh</u>ip, <u>th</u>umb, <u>ch</u>air

**Page 83**
**Row 1:** arch, beach, peach
**Row 2:** roach, coach, couch
  1. each       3. much
  2. teach     4. rich

**Page 84**
Check that all five words are written for each word wheel.
**Column 1 Word Wheel:** crack, hack, track, sack, back
**Column 2 Word Wheel:** cluck, puck, truck, luck, duck
**Column 3 Word Wheel:** dock, sock, clock, rock, lock

**Page 85**
**Row 1:** fish, brush, wash
**Row 2:** cash, hush, bush
**Adding sh:** dash, smash, mash, trash, rash, flash

**Page 86**
**Adding th:** Earth, math, teeth, tooth, bath, moth
Check that lines are drawn from words to correct pictures.

**Page 87**
**Row 1:** peach—Fill in **ch**; fish—Fill in **sh**
**Row 2:** brush—Fill in **sh**; couch—Fill in **ch**
**Row 3:** duck—Fill in **ck**; tooth—Fill in **th**
**Row 4:** cash—Fill in **sh**; truck—Fill in **ck**

**Page 88**
**Adding nch:** bench, branch, wrench
**Adding tch:** watch, hatch, patch

**Page 89**
Check that all four words are written for each word wheel:
**nch:** bunch, lunch, munch, hunch
**tch:** batch, latch, match, catch
Circle *inch.* Cross out *itch.*
Circle *itch.* Cross out *inch.*

**Page 90**
**Adding kn:** knit, knee, knot, knight, knock, knife
Check that lines are drawn from words to correct pictures.

**Page 91**
**Adding wr:** wreath, wren, wrist, write, wrap, wring
Use your wrists to <u>wring</u> out the cloth.

**Page 92**
**-ail family**
**Row 1:** mail, nail, pail
**Row 2:** sail, tail, trail
**-ain family**
**Row 1:** main, pain, rain
**Row 2:** stain, brain, chain
Circle: quail, snail, train

**Page 93**
Check that all four words are written for the word wheel: may, bay, say, day
  1. tray
  2. Today
  3. pay
  4. play
Circle: play, clay, tray, Today, birthday, pay, hay, Jay, stay, play

**Page 94**
**-eat family:** beat, meat, heat, seat—Circle *seat* (chair).
**-eal family:** deal, meal, heal, seal—Circle *seal.*
**-eam family:** team, dream, beam, seam—Circle *dream.*
**-each family:** beach, reach, peach, teach—Circle *beach.*

**Page 95**
**Column 1: eep:** deep, keep, sleep, sweep
**Column 2: eed:** feed, need, seed, weed
**Column 3: eek:** cheek, peek, seek, week

**Page 96**
**Adding ie:** tie, pie, fries
  1. lie    2. cries    3. die

**Page 97**
**Row 1:** boat, road, goat
**Row 2:** coat, soap, toast
  1. toad    2. float    3. moat

**Page 98**
Check that all four words are written for the word wheel: blue, clue, true, glue
  1. juice    3. suit
  2. fruit    4. ruin

**Page 99**
  1. stain    4. glue    7. heat
  2. tail     5. jeep
  3. play    6. goat

**Page 100**
**Row 1:** saw, jaw, paw
**Row 2:** straw, draw, claw
**Row 3:** fawn, crawl, hawk

**Page 101**
**Adding ew:** new, few, mew, dew
  1. blew
  2. chew
  3. flew
  4. screw
  5. stew

**Page 102**
**Row 1:** boil, coil, soil
**Row 2:** coin, droid, foil
**Row 3:** noise, choice, voice—Circle *choice* and *voice.*
**Row 4:** point, joint, join—Circle *point* and *joint.*

**Page 103**
**Row 1:** hook, cook, hoof
**Row 2:** cookie, hoodie
  1. book—Circle *took* and *nook.*
  2. foot—Circle *shook.*
  3. wood—Circle *good.*
  4. hood—Circle *look* and *stood.*

**Page 104**
  1. broom—room
  2. hoop—scoop
  3. balloon—cartoon
  4. moose—goose
  5. pool—school
  6. spoon—moon
  7. Boo
  8. moo

**Page 105**
**Row 1:** cloud, couch, house
**Row 2:** mouse, spout, mouth
Circle: house, mouse
Stars: *about, out,* and *shout* rhyme; *cloud, proud,* and *loud* rhyme; *found, sound,* and *round* rhyme

**Page 106**
  1. crown
  2. clown
**Adding ow:** flower, towel, tower, meow, shower

**Page 107**
  1. **Circle:** bow, arrow
  2. **Circle:** know, tow
  3. **Circle:** row, crows
  4. **Circle:** throw
  5. **Circle:** show, mow
Check the spelling of the **ow** words.

**Page 108**
**Row 1:** straw—circle **aw**; boil—circle **oi**
**Row 2:** cloud—circle **ou**; screw—circle **ew**
**oo** like **"hoop"**—*boot* and *soon*
**oo** like **"hook"**—*foot* and *wood*